Following Francis of Assisi
A Spirituality for Daily Living

Patti Normile

ST. ANTHONY MESSENGER PRESS

Cincinnati, Ohio

Scripture citations are taken from the *New Revised Standard Version Bible*, copyright ©1989 by the Division of Christian Education of the National Council of Churches of Christ in the U.S.A. and used by permission.

Excerpts from Bonaventure's *Major Life*, *The Testament of St. Francis* and "The Canticle of Brother Sun" are taken from *St. Francis of Assisi: Writings and Early Biographies*, edited by Marion A. Habig, copyright ©1973 by Franciscan Herald Press, and reprinted with permission of the publisher.

Cover and book design by Mary Alfieri
Cover illustration by Michael O'Neill McGrath, O.S.F.S.
Electronic format and pagination by Sandra Digman

ISBN 0-86716-240-6

Copyright ©1996, Patti Normile

All rights reserved.

Published by St. Anthony Messenger Press
Printed in the U.S.A.

Contents

Introduction

O N THE EVE OF OCTOBER 4, the feast of Saint
Francis of Assisi, Franciscans and friends of Saint
Francis around the world celebrate the *Transitus*, the
passing of a little poor man from life on earth to eternal
life. Throughout the world thousands revere the
memory of one who appears foolish to some, a mystery
to many, holy to multitudes.

In the gigantic basilica in Assisi, a walled city on a
hill overlooking the plains of Umbria in Italy,
thanksgiving prayers raised on the feast day express
gratitude to God for calling Francis Bernardone to a life
focused on following unflinchingly his love, Lady
Poverty, as she led him ever closer to Christ. Residents
and visitors to the stony mount revel in dances and
feasting. With banners flying, native costumes flashing
and medieval music sounding, Assisi continues more
than eight centuries of tradition by announcing to the
world that a great saint of Christendom was born
within its walls, frolicked in its streets and died loving
its people—who had loved, rejected, then loved him
again.

Francis Bernardone was born in 1182 in the
mountain town of Assisi in what is today central Italy.

He died in that same town in 1226. During the intervening forty-four years he went from riches to rags, from a position of prestige and power as the son of a wealthy merchant to being a homeless beggar—by his own choice.

Francis really did only one memorable thing with his life: He lived the gospel of Jesus Christ. This book invites you to explore the possibility of doing one memorable thing with your life: Live the gospel of Jesus Christ in the manner of Saint Francis of Assisi.

Francis was a dreamer and a visionary—a dreamer who followed the lead of his dreams, a visionary who heard God speak to him. He asked no one to follow him, but within a few years after he commenced his spiritual journey, thousands flocked after him. Had the dreams and visions he pursued been mere folly, as the townspeople of Assisi first believed, he would have been forgotten soon after his death. Instead of sinking into oblivion, two years after he died Francis was canonized a saint by the Catholic Church, and the cornerstone was laid for the mammoth basilica that rises in his name on the shoulder of Mount Subasio.

His way of following the Lord soon became a treasure in the hearts of multitudes. Nearly eight centuries after his death, Saint Francis of Assisi is revered as one of the most beloved and well-known followers of Jesus. Thousands still seek what is known as the Franciscan way of following Jesus.

"Why after you? Why after you?" Brother Masseo asked Francis. "Why does all the world run after you? You are not handsome. You have little learning and are not of noble birth. Why does all the world run after you?" (See *The Little Flowers of St. Francis*, chapter 10.) We know today that all the world does not run after Francis. Many flee from his delight in poverty and simplicity. But those who listen to his story with open hearts and minds and spirits are bound to be transformed by that experience. Many still do run after the poor little man of Assisi. Brother Masseo's "Why?" persists.

What does a saint who lived centuries ago have to offer today's men and women, particularly laypersons immersed in a culture moving toward the millennium on the wings of technology, consumerism, personal gratification and achievement? The intent of this book is to explore the mystery of Franciscan spirituality particularly as it touches the lives of laypeople. Where does Francis fit into the daily existence of those who struggle to feed and clothe and educate their families? What appeal does his way of life have for people in the marketplace—a department store clerk, a mail carrier, a college president, an oncology nurse, a widower, a student?

At the beginning of the thirteenth century Francis heard Christ speaking to him from the crucifix in the little Church of San Damiano, "Go and rebuild my Church." Francis' efforts centered first on physically rebuilding the dilapidated little churches surrounding Assisi. Then the meaning of the message was clarified: His life's mission was to rebuild the spiritual foundation of the Church.

If Christ's message to us today were to ring from a crucifix in our church, we might hear him say, "Go and rebuild your corner of the world—your family, Church, community, place of work." We are not called to rebuild the whole world in one fell swoop, just our corner of the world—beginning with our own spiritual foundation, our personal relationship with Jesus. Franciscan spirituality is the powerful tool with which we can chip away the nonessentials in our lives while constructing a spiritual foundation from which to rebuild our corner of the world.

A story is told about a sculptor who worked in Italy. He worked each day in the yard of his house. (Chiseling stone is messy work and his wife was particular about dust in the house.) A young boy appeared at the gate each day after school to watch the sculptor as he hammered and chiseled at the large chunk of stone. One day as he came for his daily visit, the boy was astonished at what he saw. He exclaimed to the sculptor (in Italian, of course), "Hey, mister, how did you know there was a lion in there?"

We know, of course, that the lion of the sculptor's art was in the mind and creativity of the artist. What we are to become is the creative work of the God who created us. When we begin to chip away at the nonessentials in our lives, we may discover to our own amazement, "There is a Franciscan in there!"

Francis was overjoyed at Brother Masseo's question about why the whole world seemed to run after him. The question acknowledged Francis as he longed to be seen—simple, sinful, poor, unattractive, ignorant, possessing no personal power. There could be but one reason for multitudes to flock to Francis: God, Francis thought, could not have chosen a more vile human to puzzle and challenge the pomp and power, intellectualism and materialism of the world. Many would follow Francis of Assisi because in the transparency of his holy humility, God's Spirit could shine through without hindrance.

That is why, eight centuries after Francis died, people still run after him. In a culture that reveres possessions we see Francis and his followers comfortable in poverty as a chosen life-style. In an era of power politics we perceive in Francis great peace in powerlessness. Amid pressure to achieve prestige in society through contrived status and its symbols, whether they be Harley Davidson T-shirts on one's body or BMWs in the driveway, we discover genuine prestige and identity in the symbol of the cross. The dignity or stature of who we are comes from following one who knew that glory cannot be found in self but only in God.

The spirituality of Francis, who chose to be lowly and humble, reaches out to us through the ages. It touches us at low points in life, when we are face-to-face with our own sinfulness and failure. It balances the times of accomplishment and success in life with the knowledge that all good comes from God. We acknowledge with the psalmist, "It is he that made us, and we are his" (Psalm 100:3b).

The spirituality of Francis of Assisi is not something added on to Christianity. Perhaps it is the essence of Christianity. Distilled from centuries of inculturation, Franciscan Christianity seeks to extract the simplicity and purity of Jesus' life and teachings and pour them into our daily lives.

The Franciscan movement has been able to

revitalize itself in each century. In the Middle Ages the Black Plague claimed many Franciscans (estimates run as high as ninety percent), because they lived among the poor, who were most afflicted. Still, the numbers of Franciscans continued to multiply. Almost everyone recognizes that something is wrong in the world today. To some this is a dismal, frightening realization. To followers of Francis, such a world circumstance reveals a glorious opportunity to reintroduce Christian values into the daily scene. As Franciscan numbers were revitalized in the Middle Ages, so can Franciscan values be reestablished at the millennium.

The way to acquire Franciscan spirituality is to seek it. We explore it in the lives of those who follow Christ in the way of Saint Francis of Assisi. Although Francis of Assisi died in 1226, new life continues to grow from his spirituality. Having found the seed of Franciscan spirituality in others, we plant it in our own lives then nurture its growth with prayer, thoughts and actions.

CHAPTER ONE

Discovering Spirituality

WHEN I WAS INVITED TO WRITE a book on Franciscan spirituality, something inside me chuckled. Perhaps it was my spirit speaking to my head, "Now you'll have to discover what spirituality really is! You've tossed it around your brain waves long enough." How true! Contemplating spirituality has caused me to sacrifice hours of sleep as well as time I had planned to devote to other endeavors. Questions flood my mind. Do I want it? Do I need it? Do I have it?

A major obstacle in writing was the realization that the more I explored my own Franciscan spirituality, the more I uncovered my deficiencies, those unsurrendered corners of my life. I wrestled with the areas of my life that have not been relinquished to what I profess as the Franciscan way to live. I don't live with the poorest of the poor. I have a lovely home, a dear family, a nice car, opportunities to travel and a myriad of material blessings. Can I really call myself "Franciscan"? I kept asking myself.

Then it came to me. The spiritual life is a journey and I am still on the road. As the saying goes, "God is not finished with me yet." What I have to share reflects my wanderings, my byroads, the many detours and dead ends, the potholes and washouts along the way. My spirituality, like yours, is traveled on the road of daily life. Francis' desire for a spiritual life was rooted in his secular life with all its abundance, vitality and gaiety. From that life grew his recognition of his need for God. Whoever we are and whatever we have are the basis of our spiritual growth.

Spirituality—what is it? Does everyone possess spirituality, while some recognize its existence in their lives and others seem oblivious to its existence? Could there be a spirituality "gene" that develops in some and not in others? I wonder whether spirituality can be "caught," inherited or offered to another person as a gift.

Is Franciscan spirituality passed along from Franciscan believer to Franciscan believer from the time of Saint Francis of Assisi until the present in a continuous line of transfer? Perhaps it has been bequeathed through the centuries like a flame nurtured and passed from person to person before kitchen matches or Bic lighter were invented. I wonder if the fire of Franciscan spirituality leaped into being the moment the lightning of the great "aha!" struck Francis. Our own "ahas" may fan that distant light into the flame of our own spirituality.

Some people seem blind to the existence of spirituality, while others are so acutely aware of the spiritual that they cannot say, "Good morning," without yielding to its mystical presence.

Is spirituality like the DNA of our biological existence—unique to each of us? Or is it like a Holy Spirit molecule—identical to all humans but lived out in dramatically different ways? We might ask whether there is an average age when spirituality "kicks in" like hormones flaring up in teenage years. Perhaps spirituality is the influence in life that creates a road map for us to follow. Since we live in a power-obsessed world, we may consider whether spirituality empowers us or weakens us by making us totally dependent on God.

Considering spirituality is a bit like savoring a new dish for the first time. You roll it around on your tongue attempting to discern what it contains—herbs, spices, cheese or wine. How is Franciscan spirituality unique? Benedictine, Dominican, Jesuit spiritualities and a myriad of others are all authentic ways of following Jesus. Which is for you?

The word *spirituality* doesn't have a particularly mysterious ring to it. Those interested in religion or spiritual matters encounter it frequently, may speak it often. But try to define it, try to grasp it and make it your own, then it becomes elusive and tries to wiggle away from our understanding. Defining spirituality is akin to expressing the inexpressible.

Webster's makes an attempt to define it: "incorporeal quality or state; spirit-mindedness; that which belongs to the church...or to religion." Definitions derive from the world of the intellect and limit the realm of spiritual terms. Spirituality enfolds body and mind while moving beyond those tangible parts of our being into the spiritual world, where words may limit rather than encompass.

Spirituality is not a belief system, but rather our basic approach to life. It might be contrasted with the extent to which the material or intellectual worlds provide a foundation to our approach to life. Spirituality encompasses our religious, moral, sacred and secular values, the way we think and pray and live. Spirituality is the skeletal system on which religious beliefs and practices take flesh. Because spirituality is so all-encompassing, it can be difficult to pin down in verbal terms.

In *The Third Order Vocation Book*, Fathers Jovian Weigel, O.F.M., and Leonard Foley, O.F.M., state: "A spirituality is a particular way or emphasis in following Christ.... [M]any things...are common to all Christians, and these are more important than the interests of any one group of Christians: Christlike love and forgiveness, community, personal and communal prayer, celebration of the sacramental life of the Church, obedience to legitimate authority, love of Scripture, concern for justice and peace.... But there can be a difference in what can only be called emphasis. We speak of a Benedictine, a Dominican, a Franciscan spirituality. There is a spirituality proper to laypeople, as contrasted with that of priest, or that of nuns or brothers."

My childhood memories relate to the complexity of defining spirituality. Once I accidentally broke a thermometer at Grandma's house. Trying to gather the mercury balls that raced around the tabletop was an impossible challenge for young fingers. The concept of spirituality is like one of those silver beads of mercury that spilled from the fractured vial. Understanding rolls this way and dashes that way, taking us always on a new course—sometimes toward the edge, always in an unexpected direction. To gather all the shining elements of spirituality into a single unit is neither possible nor desirable. We must allow it to roll into every aspect of life.

Another memory is of gathering and opening milkweed pods. As a breeze brushed the pale, plumelike parachutes of the seeds, they soared away. Once loose, they could not be replaced in the pod. To repack a milkweed pod would stifle the new growth potential. Like mercury scurrying from a broken thermometer, like silken seeds wafting from a milkweed pod, the concept of spirituality evades attempts to contain it in words or specific concrete thoughts. Therefore, in considering spirituality, we must be content with ambiguity.

I cannot define spirituality for you. You cannot interpret it for your spouse or child or friend. The best beginning we can make in wrapping our minds around spirituality is to acknowledge it as a vital though unseen power in life. With that understanding we begin to explore our own lives, the lives of the great saints and the lives of those holy ones we know who may never be canonized by the Church. These are lives guided by the unseen yet dynamic force of the spiritual life. Within these lives lie seeds of spirituality.

Spirituality develops from living Jesus' question, "But who do you say that I am?" (Mark 8:29b). Our response to Jesus will be reflected in our everyday life—the choices we make, the sacrifices we undergo. This book is not intended to contradict your spirituality but to offer an expanded view of what spirituality means in your life. This book is about taking our spirituality from the pews of our churches and investing it in our workplaces, our homes, our communities, our hearts.

The young search for ways to fit God into their lives. The old seek understanding of where God is, perhaps where God hides, in their present circumstances. Exploring spirituality is our way to those answers.

In his book *Holiness*, Donald Nicholl states two concepts about holiness that are equally true of spirituality, which targets holiness as its goal. He declares that holiness is, "an area in which practice is everything and theory is nothing." He continues, "...[O]ne truly holy person is worth more than any number of books about holiness." No need to toss this book aside, however. It only indicates that whatever is said here can never be yours until it is put into practice. Consider an airline pilot: Would you prefer to fly with one who has read a multitude of flight manuals but never flown a plane, or one who has both read the manuals and practiced flying skills again and again and again?

I once took a few golf lessons from a wise pro. After he had me hitting long and straight with great consistency, he said, "Now, hit ten thousand balls and that shot will be yours." If we seek the meaning of spirituality, we must search for a spiritual person whose direction we can follow. When we discover a model for our spirituality, we will practice in ten thousand ways living in faithfulness to that spirituality. Then it will be ours. As we discover its meaning and practice its message, we in turn become spiritual models for others—not to imitate but to follow in their own ways in their own lives.

Caution is advised in seeking a spirituality for our lives. We must not become like a fish who wonders what water is and goes in search of it outside the pond. If we cannot discover spirituality in our everyday life, we cannot find it anywhere.

There are good spiritualities as well as those that are not good. Good spirituality leads us to God. It provides the energy that empowers activities toward goodness. Good spirituality brings us the gifts of the Spirit: wisdom, understanding, right judgment, courage, knowledge, reverence and awe. Good spirituality bears the fruits of the Spirit: love, peace, joy, kindness, goodness, patience, perseverance, gentleness, faith, truthfulness, self-control, chastity. Spirituality is what we follow in the dark of unknowing or difficulty that leads us to the light of peace and understanding. The destiny of good spirituality is holiness. We will leave the destiny of bad spirituality to its own designs.

Why Franciscan Spirituality?

Conversations with many who claim Franciscan spirituality as a way of life reveal a common origin. "I met a Franciscan friar who changed my life around," Pat says with gratitude. "Franciscan sisters taught me in school. I'll always remember how much they loved me and the good Lord," Genny remembers. "We move a lot and we always look for a Franciscan church because the friars are so humble and kind...so near to God," John claims. Few people initially say that they gravitated to a Franciscan life-style because of laypersons they met. Yet further discussion reveals that laypersons who follow Saint Francis have also been vital in the ongoing conversion process.

It is regrettable that laypersons are not recognized more often as models of Saint Francis of Assisi. The absence of a clearly identifiable Franciscan charism in the laity of our time is indeed a void in spiritual history. Francis himself began his spiritual journey as a layman. He became a deacon, but was never ordained to the priesthood. The Franciscan identity of the laypeople who followed his Christian way was so well defined that some call it a major factor in the downfall of feudalism. The collapse of that system, which bonded humans in serfdom, was hastened by the refusal of Francis' followers to bear arms in support of feudal lords.

In a time when the diminishing number of priests is a concern for the Church, the potential of the laity within society is a sign of hope for the future. Faithful followers of Saint Francis grace our parishes, our communities, our schools and workplaces.

Lack of a clear identity may be responsible for the failure to recognize laity as models of Franciscan spirituality. Franciscan friars and sisters spend their lives being formed in Franciscan spirituality. (More than one friar has confessed his longing for ordination in order to be "finished"—only to learn that ordination is only the beginning of the spiritual journey.)

Ongoing spiritual formation is like creating a braid. One begins with varied strands of life—self, God, other people, work, prayer, joy, pain. These intertwine one with the other as we examine their spiritual meaning in our lives. As they are plaited together, the whole becomes stronger. New fibers—events of our lives—are integrated into the plaited creation. The process continues. This formation procedure is expected of Franciscan brothers, sisters and fathers. When the result of the process is witnessed in one's life-style, it bears an identity. It is known as Franciscan.

Laypeople, on the other hand, are encountered without the identity associated with friars or sisters. Members of the Secular Franciscan Order (formerly called the Third Order of St. Francis) may have an identity as "Franciscan" within their communities, but most do not possess a distinct, visible identity outside of those associations.

This book invites laypersons to follow the way of Saint Francis of Assisi. A strengthened concept of your own spirituality will help establish an identity that says, "My life is focused on Jesus in the manner of Saint Francis." By clarifying our Franciscan identity, we enhance our ability to articulate the Franciscan mission of our lives. Franciscan spirituality will have a face—your face, my face—as it becomes visible to those who search for deeper meaning in life.

Be careful not to confuse identity with a label. A label is an external designation affixed to something. Labels define and limit; labels stamp people and items with characteristics that another person thinks they possess. Identity, on the other hand, grows from within. Identity is limitless in its potential. Identity evolves from who we are deep within our beings.

The Call of Franciscan Spirituality

The United States of America is speckled with hospitals, colleges, towns and cities bearing names which witness to Saint Francis of Assisi—San Francisco, St. Francis Hospital, Francisville, St. Francis Village, St. Francis College, S. François. The name of the saint is stamped on maps and highway signs. But is it stamped on our way of life?

It is amazing that many who live in a society that desires to be rich follow a fellow who wished to be poor. It is puzzling that many follow one who chose to be simple when complexity marks our era. Why seek the way of a humble one when pride is often today's trademark? The answer is simple: Amid all the complexity and avarice of contemporary society, many recognize a call to live a life-style that draws them closer to God. That way of life is one that follows Christ as Francis did—humbly, obediently, joyfully. Francis discovered that material wealth holds no lasting joy— temporary pleasure or momentary happiness, perhaps, but no sustained joy. Complexity confuses our values. Pride puffs us up and separates us from others.

Personal Journeys

I did not choose Franciscan spirituality. Francis of Assisi chose me. As a young teacher, I had saved every cent I could to travel to Europe to explore the countries about which I taught. Our tour group visited Assisi during the busy summer months. A brief stop in Assisi changed the course of my life in spite of the fact that the tour director had claimed, "Assisi is just a 'pit stop' on our way to more important sights."

Umbria basked in the warmth of a sunny July day as we approached the mountain town looming above the plain. The mammoth Basilica of San Francesco seemed to be sculpted from the mountain. Strangely, no other tourist busses dotted the parking area of the Basilica that day. We moved into the cool, dim interior of the upper church. The miracle of its construction in the thirteenth century in just two years is a feat that would daunt the giants of modern construction technology. We viewed and admired paintings by Giotto. I babbled on, revealing my minimal knowledge of art of the period. Then we descended to the tomb of Francis in the lower church. Franciscan spirituality grabbed me for the first time in my life.

I gazed at the massive pillar of stone holding the tomb in which the saint's body rests. I wondered at the iron cord that binds the coffin. As I stood beneath the body of Francis, a force like that of a powerful magnet in my heart seemed to bind me to that iron bar. The tour group moved on, but I could not leave. Nor did I want to depart. A friend returned to the area of the tomb to say that the tour was leaving. I stood rooted to the stone floor. She took my arm and physically led me away to an impatient group of tourists waiting on the bus. A great sorrow shadowed my departure. No words echoed in my head, but an intense longing called me to remain in that hallowed place to learn what I had not yet discovered.

During our descent from the city on the hill, I craned my neck to absorb a lasting visual image of the Basilica. That image and a blurred photo were my remembrances for years while I mentally explored the mystery of those compelling moments at the tomb of Francis.

The experience was beyond comprehension at the time. Though beyond thought, it was rooted deep in my spirit. Looking back over the years, I realize that a dynamic spiritual call had sounded within me. No words echoed at the tomb. No spiritual wisdom flowed from my thoughts. But the spirit of Francis in Christ held me in that sacred place long enough to imprint in my heart a desire to seek the source of the call.

I would like to report that I immediately set out in search of understanding. I did not. I simply kept the experience, treasured it, pondered it. The next year I converted to the Catholic faith. I cannot say that conversion was an active, ongoing element in my daily life. Becoming Catholic was something I had done, past tense. For nearly a dozen years life went on as usual until the experience of Assisi was renewed on meeting Franciscan friars at a retreat center near my home. The spirit that called at the tomb of Saint Francis now had feet and hands, a voice and heart, all of which invited me to a new life—a spiritual life. The search was on.

That was my call; for others the call came in different ways.

Gloria's call to Franciscan life came via a fluttering, yellow flyer she chased up a windy city street. Risking life and limb, she dodged cars in the drenching rain before planting her foot firmly on the paper. The newspaper woman claims it is the only such fly-away paper she ever felt inspired to chase and pick up. The flyer told about living Franciscan life as a layperson. No name or address was on the paper, so Gloria's next task was to seek its source. When she asked a friend about Franciscan life, the woman replied, "You don't want to get mixed up with *that*! It's a very strict and hard life to live. It's for the old folks, I think. They pray a lot. It's for people who don't have anything else to do!" So, like the rich young man of Scripture who decided he had better things to do (see Matthew 19:16-22), Gloria went on with her daily life. The call of the fluttering yellow paper had a long wait before Gloria would follow its nudging.

Twenty-four years later a Franciscan mission calendar reminded Gloria of her earlier interest in Franciscan life. She discovered the Secular Franciscan Order and began a formation process in Franciscan spirituality. Her friend was right in part: Franciscan life is for people who pray a lot. It is for people who have nothing more important to do—nothing more important than seeking God's way in their life. Franciscan life may be hard to live. As for being strict, the Franciscan way is freeing rather than restricting. The Franciscan way frees us from the nonessentials of life, allows us to focus on what is fundamental to Christian life.

Stories of Saint Francis' life changed Gloria's life dramatically. One of the most significant for her was Francis' encounter with the leper. Francis, who loved beautiful things, had a particular aversion to those whose bodies were ravaged by leprosy. Many people with the disease roamed the countryside around Assisi. After his conversion, Francis encountered one of them as he rode along. Overcome with compassion, he leaped from his horse, and to his own astonishment, he embraced and kissed the man.

This account reminds Gloria that we must all face our "lepers"—the ugly sides of ourselves. She asks herself, "Who or what are my 'lepers'? Whom am I avoiding? Whom do I need to embrace? What am I afraid of?" Gloria is puzzled that she waited a quarter of a century to discover Franciscan spirituality. She would do it all over again, searching longer and harder if necessary. The effects of Franciscan spirituality make the search and the endeavor seem like small sacrifices.

Ron first met Francis in a friend's garden. The saint stood next to a birdbath in his concrete habit. The bird population that perched on him had unceremoniously decorated his stony garb. Ron is grateful that their relationship did not end there. A "birdbath" Franciscan spirituality is as limited as a "sweet baby Jesus" Christianity. The nativity Jesus, swaddled and lying in the clean, warm straw, is only the beginning (and perhaps an inaccurate image) of the Christian journey. Francis' love for all of nature is only one aspect of a many-faceted spirituality that leads to the Franciscan way of following Jesus.

Leaving Comfort Behind

Resistance can stand between us and our pursuit of spirituality. That resistance finds roots in the fear of facing what a defined spiritual life may demand of us. The intangible nature of the spiritual life may appear irrelevant in a pragmatic world that accepts what is tangible, graspable, material. We read the lives of the saints and learn of pain and suffering, which may not be attractive to us. Realization dawns that yielding to spirituality demands sacrifice. This awareness alienates some from the journey toward the spiritual life.

Once I was awed by the view from the hotel balcony at a vacation spot—ocean on one side and the sound on the other. Ribbons of birds laced the sky and sea in search of sustenance. Watching the surf hurl itself on the beach as dozens of dolphins trolled the waters, stopping for an occasional *pas de deux* on the surface, I experienced no desire to leave this vantage point and venture to the beach. The comfort of my location, the beauty of the view, the panorama from the elevated balcony were satiating. I did not want to wander down to the shore or wade in the incoming tide or watch the dolphins blow their plumes a dozen feet from me. I was too comfortable.

Our spirituality can be like that experience. We arrive at a place in life that is spiritually comfortable. We go to church, say our prayers, receive the sacraments. Even with such meaningful spiritual realities in our lives, we may be standing on the balcony of the spiritual life rather than plunging into its depths. We may be leading a spectator life rather than actively living a life sparked by our spirituality.

Fear and comfort fetter us to our safe havens. We fear the cost of plunging into new levels of spirituality. We cling tenaciously to the comfort our present life provides. The human instinct is to attach like barnacles to security and physical comfort. That human instinct provides for physical survival without reckoning with spiritual security. Your security and comfort levels may be less than or greater than your neighbor's. It matters not. Attachment to comforts and security is the key that locks us into where we are, keeping us from spiritual freedom.

Spirituality Rooted in the Secular

The sound of his horse's hooves softly clomping back up the road to the upper city were music to Francis' ears. Sitting high on the fine horse his father had given him reminded him of the elevated position his family maintained in Assisi. They were not nobility, but they were the next best thing—respected members of the wealthy merchant class. Francis was returning from delivering a bolt of fine cloth to be sewn into a wedding gown for a lovely young woman of Assisi. Whom would he marry someday? Francis pondered the thought, and it inspired a smile on his craggy face. He knew he wasn't the most handsome young man in town, but he was fun! And being the son of a wealthy father opened his prospects for marriage to include most eligible girls.

The cadence of his horse matched his family's life. Life in the Bernardone home was marked by regular rhythms. Lady Pica, who had left her native Provence to marry Pietro, supervised the Bernardone home. She cooked special dishes for the men in her life and brought a touch of gentleness and charity to the family. She created lovely embroidery for herself and to give as gifts. Francis' father dutifully tended his shop, except when he journeyed north to purchase fabrics in distant markets. His younger brother bothered and puzzled Francis—bothered him when he wanted to tag along with Francis and his friends, puzzled him because his brother seemed so different from him.

The weekly rhythm of life in Assisi was punctuated by church bells. The Bernardones walked as a family through the cobbled narrow streets to celebrate with the Christian community of Assisi each and every Sunday. No Saturday night revelry was an excuse for being absent. Francis' father would not have tolerated it; his mother would have anguished in his absence.

A lark fluttered from the field beside the road, startling his horse, which broke into a trot. The new rhythm of horse and rider shifted Francis' thoughts. He laughed aloud. He had been thinking of marriage, and he was too young to be considering marriage! He had lots of living to do! At a touch of Francis' heels his spirited steed broke into a rolling canter up the sloping road to town. The coins Francis had received for the cloth jingled in the leather pouch at his hip.

Glancing over his shoulder, Francis was glad he lived in the elevated town. His father had impressed him with the responsibilities of being among the town's privileged people. He liked to look down upon the forests and roads through which Assisi might be attacked should the Perugians or other enemies choose to wage war. Francis experienced a sense of paternal pride for the town, knowing that he would be among its defenders in such an event. In the meantime he and his friends had plans for an evening of song and some wine tonight. Francis was following in his father's footsteps to become a business success, a leader in the community.

We naturally follow in the ways of those close to us in our early lives. I recall walking in knee-deep snow as a small child. It was rough going for short legs. But when I was with Mom and Dad, it became easier. I could step in their footprints, which pressed places for my next steps. Sometimes their strides were too long for little legs. Real stretching was required to keep up. They would stop and wait for me. I would follow.

For Leonard, God seemed to leave his life when his father died when he was a teenager. He loved his dad deeply. He had planned to model his life after his dad. With his world shattered, Leonard ceased trusting God. He stopped attending church. Later, while serving in the military, he found a friend who sensed Leonard's need to return to a spiritual life. Each Sunday morning the friend would sit and stare at Leonard in his bed. He vowed to continue this persistent ritual until Leonard would get up some morning and go to Mass. Dogged by his friend's persistence, that day came for Leonard. The two friends were greeted at a small military chapel by a Franciscan friar. The experience of God's forgiveness through the friar's ministry led Leonard to seek Franciscan principles for his way of life. He now serves as formation director for Secular Franciscans.

On our spiritual journeys we need someone to follow—a path-finder to lead the way. Mentors, teachers, spiritual companions, parents help us find the way. We must always challenge where our pathfinders are leading us. Spirituality activates life's energy toward good and toward God.

Francis never sat down with the Franciscan Planning Committee to develop a systematic program for being Franciscan. He did not take pen in hand to create a definitive work entitled *Franciscan Spirituality*. Instead, he took the difficult path to revealing

Franciscan spirituality: He lived it! Franciscan spirituality emerged from Francis' total commitment to God. He weighed his every action against the gospel message. When he found his way wanting, as he most often did, he took the gospel message back into his daily living to use it to chisel away all that was not of God. Gospel to life, life to the gospel—he tossed one to the other until they became one in him.

From his years of endeavor to merge the gospel with his life, there surfaced recognizable strands that would become known as Franciscan spiritual qualities: chosen radical poverty; oneness with God, others and nature; acceptance of suffering; a deep desire for peace that allows no one to be an enemy; joy and praise to God in everything. Francis did write Rules for his followers. These Rules, rather than being specific steps to follow exactly, paint a picture of how to live gospel life simply and faithfully.

Saint Clare claimed, "Christ is the way and Francis showed it to me." Francis continues to reveal Christ as the way to all who seek him. Sister Thea Bowman, a Franciscan sister dying of cancer, declared, "I have tried to make a day-by-day decision that I want to live joyfully. I want to be good news to other people, so I try to laugh, to smile. I try to find the source of inner joy and strength" (*Catholic Digest*, "Words for Quiet Moments," March 1994). Franciscan spirituality for laypeople is woven into relationships. It surrounds us at work, shaping ethics and attitudes to those of Christ. Spirituality carves the leisure moments of life so that joy rises from the pleasure of these times. Spirituality is not separated from our daily life; it is the warp and woof of our everyday existence.

For anyone seeking Christ, Francis provides a challenging but unfailing path. Though Francis died in 1226, new life continues to grow from his spiritual legacy to Christians. We are invited to become part of the legacy of Franciscan spirituality. We can pass on our faith and Franciscanism simply by being who we are.

CHAPTER TWO

Surrender and Conversion

THE FALLING OF AUTUMN LEAVES resembles
conversion. First their color changes. Then a few
begin to fall. Not all tumble to earth at once; the tree
seems a bit reluctant to release its robe of leaves. But the
flurry of falling foliage continues. Finally summer's
greenery and autumn's vibrant finery is shed and the
branches of the tree stand stark against the wintry sky.

Francis' conversion progressed through stages that
altered the color of his life. The vision of God's purpose
in his life unfolded through a series of visions. He who
had thought he was far from ready for marriage
suddenly fell madly in love—in love with Lady Poverty.
With this adoration Francis sacrificed his desire for his
earthly father's wealth.

Another dream caused him to surrender the quest
for fame. Marching off to fight what he believed to be a
just battle, Francis awakened to a voice in the night. The
voice challenged him: Did he wish to serve the Lord or
the servant? He chose the Lord. Little did he realize at
that moment in the night what surrender and sacrifice
would be required as he shed the protective leaves of
his early life. He would sacrifice his home, his family,
his friends, his former life. He would surrender his

former image of himself—the vibrant, radiant youth beloved by most of the townsfolk. (Even those who grumbled about his flamboyant life-style secretly cherished Francis' zest for life.)

Confused and befuddled, Francis wandered through the countryside of Assisi—diving into the solitude of mountain caves to seek understanding, basking on rocky hillsides in attempts to warm the chill of his aloneness with the sun's rays. Then one day he stumbled into the little chapel of San Damiano. Bending low under the burden of indecision, bowing to the Christ on the crucifix, Francis experienced deep in his spirit a thundering command. "Francis, go and rebuild my church, which, as you can see, is falling into ruin!"

"Ah," Francis thought, "an answer to my search!" He now had a task to perform—one he understood. He was being called to do something. He could use his hands, his mind, his feet, even his father's money to carry out this order, which emanated from the crucified figure.

In the months ahead, Francis patched and mended abandoned chapels dotting the landscape below Assisi with borrowed, bought and begged stones. Airy roofs were closed to the elements. Francis could look at his work and feel a sense of pride in the re-creation of God's houses. This pride was soon to be sacrificed with Francis' realization that physical reconstruction was not his call. He was to yield himself to God and to the awesome task of rebuilding the spiritual foundation of the Church of Christendom.

When his father, Pietro Bernardone, demanded that Francis return to him those material things that Francis had taken for his work on the churches, Francis shed the final traces of the summer of his life. What a crowd that family disagreement gathered in the piazza of the Bishop's house! How astonished they were when Francis returned his father's possessions—including the clothes from his back.

More difficult to understand is Francis returning Pietro's fatherhood to him. "Until now I called you my father, but now I can say without reserve, 'Our Father who art in heaven.' He is all my wealth and I place all my confidence in him" (Saint Bonaventure, *Major Life*, chapter 4). Harsh as this action was, it reveals Francis' decision to allow no one but God to control his life. Having lived with his father for two decades, Francis knew the man's will to control his business endeavors, community issues and his family. To remain faithful to the path he was following, Francis chose another Father to follow. Shedding possessions, power and prestige, Francis stood, like the tree of late autumn, stark and naked before the world. As his faith journey progressed, Francis would allow no one and nothing control over his life—not others' opinions, not family or friends, not pain or illness, not hunger, not ridicule or rejection, not fame—only God.

We live in a culture where control is a factor to be grappled with. We have the power to control many issues that affect us. Ours is an intensely mobile society that provides many options about where we live and work. Adequate incomes permit many to make choices in education and occupation according to their desires rather than inherit their parents' trade as they would have a few generations ago. The medical profession provides us with the ability to control our health through knowledge of proper diet, exercise, mental attitude and medical treatment. Thermostats in home, office, and even in our cars enable us to control our atmosphere without waiting for the whims of a cool breeze or the warming sun.

We have become accustomed to creature comforts that would have been unthinkable fifty to a hundred years ago. What is a luxury in one generation becomes a "necessity" to the next. I recall a young niece clearing the dinner table at my parents' house. She looked around the kitchen with a puzzled look and then exclaimed, "There's no dishwasher!" A generation earlier, when I was a small child visiting a great-grandmother, my astonished discovery was, "There's no bathroom!" For the next generation it may be, "There's no computer!" or "There's no dome over your yard!"

Families are often created by the choices of very young people who decide to marry (or bear children while unmarried) without consent of or arrangement by their parents. The ravages of floods, the devastation of tornadoes or earthquakes, the destruction of drought astonish us because we are used to controlling so many elements of life. Life appears to be simultaneously highly controlled yet quite out-of-control.

Loss of control sometimes results in violent reactions. Workers deprived of jobs return to the workplace armed and attacking. The demise of a major corporation leaves in its wake divorces, suicides and mental breakdowns as former employees lose their job security. Prisoners explode under rigid control in security facilities. Genocide rakes nations as perpetrators of age-old hatreds attempt to eliminate those who have controlled them. Control is a major factor in contemporary society.

Francis refused to relinquish control in his life to anyone but God, who became "my God and my all." The choices Francis made to remove from his life the control that separated him from God were not easy. Sacrifice was required to strip away what was masked as good but in reality was control by someone or something other than God.

Surrender and sacrifice were not high on the list of popular activities in Assisi in the early thirteenth century. Few considered Francis anything but foolish at best or mad or an ingrate at worst. Surrender and sacrifice are not popular concepts in today's culture, either. To some, surrender and sacrifice indicate failure and weakness. To Francis, surrender and sacrifice were not chosen ideals in his first two decades. He was a son of privilege, unaccustomed to sacrifice. He yearned to become a victorious soldier for whom surrender was unthinkable. Even as a young man Francis sensed the personal power he possessed as a result of his station in life. Money, fame and power were clearly within his grasp. He sensed that others gravitated to these elements that were available to him.

Yet surrender and sacrifice are essential elements in conversion. These factors opened Francis' path to conversion. The stark, bare tree of winter was already undergoing interior growth. Buds of new life focused on God were growing in Francis' spirit. He would have new friends, devoted ones who chose to follow Christ as he did in poverty of body, mind and spirit. He would be blessed with a new family bonded by the Body and Blood of Christ. His possessions would not be tangibles, but spiritual valuables that can be possessed only by relinquishing desire for all that is not in God's will.

Had Francis refused to make God his all, the world would have had for a few decades a successful businessman in a small town in Umbria. But it would not have had a Saint Francis of Assisi. Had an Albanian religious sister refused to make God her all, the world would have had for a few decades an excellent schoolteacher in a school for privileged young women in India. But the world would not have had a Mother Teresa of Calcutta. If you refuse to make God your all, the world will have an individual who was inspired by the Holy Spirit to explore the possibility of making God her or his all. But if you refuse, the world will not have a new saint (even with a small *s*) from your hometown.

The pursuit of the spiritual life will leave us standing naked, if not before the bishop, at least before God and ourselves. Like Adam and Eve, who suddenly realized they were naked in the garden, that possibility is an uncomfortable one for us. We are accustomed to being clothed with garments of respectability: knowledge, family rank, social standing, Church affiliation, employment status, such symbols of success as cars and neighborhoods and attire. Stripped of those physically or spiritually, we must face ourselves as God created us without the camouflage of culture or disguise.

Where to begin the process presents a challenge. God did not become all to Francis in one flash of devotion. His conversion began with simple actions. Rebuilding the ramshackle chapels around Assisi was not God's ultimate calling for Francis, but it was an essential first step. His immediate action represented his response to God. Francis did not pause to compute how many tons of stone the projects would require, where he would get the cash to commence, whose donkey would haul the rock or who might assist him in a tough construction job. He simply began to do what he had heard God request of him. His actions were his "Yes!" His move toward holiness would be long and often confusing. His holiness—and ours—is made of the scraps and fragments of life's struggles. Holiness is not a seamless garment; it is a carefully pieced quilt stitched together by the threads of our spirituality.

Falling Into the Abyss

A man was repeatedly plagued by the same dream. In the dream, he was pursued across fields by a man he recognized as his grandfather. This grandfather had died when the man was a young boy. He was remembered as a huge, gruff, distant man whom the dreamer had feared. In the dream as the man ran with the grandfather gaining on him, he would reach the edge of a precipice. With terror in his heart he would look back at the feared grandfather reaching toward him and then ahead at the cliff and impending doom. At this point he would wake up trembling, fearful, drenched in sweat. The dream became such a source of concern and disruption that the man went to a counselor. After listening to his account of the dream's terror, the counselor advised, "The next time this dream occurs, allow yourself to fall over the edge of the cliff. If you wake up before you do that, allow your imagination to carry you over the edge of the precipice."

A few nights later the dream occurred once again. By sheer force of will, the man allowed himself to fall over the edge of the cliff. Just as he did so, the huge, threatening man chasing him caught up with him. At the last instant as he fell toward the abyss, the old man reached out with his strong, brawny arms and grabbed the man. Drawing him back from the brink of danger, the old man wrapped his arms around the dreamer and whispered, "I have always wanted to hold you and love you, my child."

God pursues each of us throughout life. Before we come to know him, we may fear his power or what he may require of us. Like the man who did not really know the grandfather he feared, we run away. Francis attempted to escape from God's call. He ran through the cobbled streets of Assisi with his carefree friends without even realizing he was running from God. We may attempt to escape God's call by running through life harried by status-seeking, hyperactivity, workaholism or any of the other destructive "isms." We may not know the God who pursues us.

Madeline was a young woman who seemed to have it all. She had a law school degree, extended study abroad and service as a congressional aide. She had a passel of friends, and a variety of passions—perhaps too many passions, she claims. She also had a God whom she believed loved her—but only when she was good. And she wasn't always good. She had too many tempting opportunities to be otherwise. Alcohol and drugs prescribed for mental illness mingled until her life crumbled. She began to think that life was not worth living and contemplated suicide. Then an experience in church brought her face-to-face with God's love and her own worth.

Madeline will be the first to admit that her earlier approach to Christianity was rather lukewarm. She went through the motions as a churchgoer, contributing time and money to church activities. But her heart was invested in the supposed pleasures of life. Her commitment to God was neither hot nor cold, perhaps because she believed God loved her only when she was good. Madeline found a new definition of "good." She now measures her self-worth by how much God loves her, not by how good she is.

As a youth, Francis had a great desire—a passion— for the rousing company of his friends, the finery afforded him by his father's business, the feel of a fine horse beneath him. Then a greater passion touched his life. In his search for meaning in life, Francis wandered into the little chapel of San Damiano. A life-sized crucifix seemed bound to the chapel stone wall by cobwebs. Yet through the dust of disuse, in the dim light of the sacred place, the power of Jesus' passion changed all the passions of Francis' life: "Go and rebuild my Church, which, as you can see, is falling into ruin." Francis' lifelong response to this experience and to each new experience of God was, "My God and my all!" He now needed only God for his joy to be complete. While Francis had been a happy man before his experience before the crucifix, now he began to attain the joy that would be synonymous with his name for centuries to come.

In the little chapel of San Damiano, Francis

somehow leaped over the precipice and allowed God to grasp him. He commenced to explore the love God had reached out to wrap him in. In order for us to experience God as our all, we must begin to let go of other passions that tug at us. Some people acknowledge that they fear letting God into their lives. If God becomes their "all," they fear what sacrifice may be entailed. The dream of the fleeing man reminds us that we need not fear being caught by God. God's great desire is to love us.

After his conversion Francis always referred to himself as a great sinner and rejoiced that God could use such a one for his work. Francis even referred to himself as vile, but he knew that God loved him just as he was. He was God's good creation. If a "good" suit meets with a bowl of clam chowder, it does not mean that it is no longer our "good" suit. It simply needs some cleaning up. If we, God's good creations, are sullied by sin, we remain God's good creations. We are, however, in great need of cleansing. Francis recognized that only the redeeming love of Jesus can clean up the soil of a self-centered life.

We cannot presume to judge the spiritual vitality of the Bernardone family, yet it is fair to say it was more tepid than that of their son, Francis. Much of the Christian world follows a timid, tepid way toward Christ. Jesus' message is heard with the ears but often not followed with the heart and life-energy of the hearer. Francis had heard the message of the gospel numerous times before it settled into his being. His tepid Christianity was transformed to a boiling desire to follow and to serve his Lord.

CHAPTER THREE

'Go and Rebuild'

MARLA IS BRIGHT, ENERGETIC, ambitious and, from all appearances, successful. She has been honored for the contributions she has made to her community through volunteer endeavors. She is a regular churchgoer. She confesses that she used to play a little game with herself: She attempted to get her name and her accomplishments into area newspapers at least once a month. But she was not happy. She could not find peace in her life. A harried schedule coupled with self-centered goals clouded her chances for contentment.

When she heard the story about Francis' conversion during a retreat, Marla immediately dismissed it as a fable about a fool. But the image of the crucifix speaking to Francis would not leave her thoughts. In the weeks that followed, the crucifix seemed to speak to her: "What are you building, my Church or yourself?"

Marla's life began to change. Her past accomplishments now looked like fallen leaves. She felt naked, standing in the shadow of fleeting fame with dry and crumbling leaves of past glory swirling about her feet. She had done no blatant evil; she believes that she simply failed to do good for the right reasons.

Since her conversion experience, Marla's focus has gradually moved from herself to God. Today she is at peace. She still experiences success, but now it is focused on building the Church in her corner of the world rather than on self-gratification. She doesn't call it success. She calls it grace because God gives her opportunities to rebuild Church and community through her work and her family and her social life.

When Marla struggles with pride, she remembers, "I am an instrument God chooses to use to rebuild those crumbly places in my little space in the world. I like it that way. When I get puffed up with my accomplishments, it pushes other people and even God away. Francis helped me discover a new way."

Marla realizes that she still drifts from God. She describes conversion as being like the ebb and flow of the tide: We move toward God with all the energy of waves approaching the beach. When the pull of temptation draws us back to the deep, we begin to flounder. Then the tide of mercy once again draws us to God.

As conversion drew Francis closer to God, he also discovered God's presence in others. People with leprosy were no longer repugnant to him. He and his brothers tended their wounds. The most difficult Francis cared for himself. His love for God called him to reach out to others.

Building Community

A young woman thoroughly enjoyed her visit to a small town where friends and neighbors had gathered for a bridal shower for her friend. "Where I live, I don't even know my next-door neighbor," she complained. "I've tried to be friendly, but when I approach she just walks away. It's really lonely."

Tom and Chris were delighted when Anne spoke to them after Mass. "We're rather new in town. We've been coming to St. Isolation for several weeks, but we have met no one. We smile and say hi, but people just keep on walking." One morning after Chris joined Anne's prayer group, the group discussed their parish's welcome to newcomers and old-timers alike. Several others had joined the parish recently and had experienced the same lonely-in-a-crowd feeling.

"We had so much to do when we first moved here that we couldn't get involved in parish activities right away," Maryann said. "But we sure would have liked to have people greet us in the beginning."

Susannah added, "Everyone seems to be in such a hurry between the church door and the parking lot. I wish we could just take a few minutes after Mass to be Church to each other. We could get to know people we don't contact through other activities. We shouldn't be strangers in church."

We are all aware of the blessed strengths as well as the shortcomings of our churches, our neighborhoods and various groups with which we congregate. In those places where our lives touch others'—places where two or more gather in the Lord's name—lies the possibility of becoming Church. The objective may not be formal worship, but sharing life's events within the bonds of friendship can lead to prayer and praise among God's people. Individuals cease to be strangers when they recognize one another as brothers and sisters in Christ.

Thus Church and world are rebuilt.

Francis never knew a stranger. Gregarious even before his conversion, he greeted everyone as a brother or sister after his call from God. He hailed each one he met along the way with the greeting, *"Buon giorno!"* He even hailed his father's friends, who scorned him. He often accompanied his greeting with a sweeping gesture, a low bow—a remnant from the days he mimicked the troubadours, who acted with regal elegance as they sang the ballads he loved.

Once he fell humbly at the feet of a woman when they met at a fountain early one morning. He wanted to treat her as he saw her: as a temple of the Lord's own Spirit. But the experience so unnerved her that Francis thereafter refrained from falling to the earth in front of people. He simply pictured in his mind the Spirit of Jesus living within those he met and greeted them with great love.

Far from Assisi one fall day, Francis heard a group approaching him around a curve in the road. As they came into sight, he shouted his hello with joyful welcome. The small band returned his cordial greeting by seizing him bodily. They groped at his tunic, looking for his purse, but he had none. Angered by his poverty, they jostled him from one to another, insulting him with every shove. Tiring of their game, they hurled Francis into the bushes beside the road. Had they listened as they hastened on their way, boasting of their strength while chastising Francis for having no coins, they might have heard his cheerful call: *"Addio, amicos!* Good-bye, my friends!"

Fear creates strangers. On a visit to the city, my

friends and I realized that our parking meter was expiring. I volunteered to return to the car and feed the meter. I decided to take a shortcut through the inner-city streets. As I walked I realized that I was in unfamiliar territory. Abandoned buildings surrounded me. People who had lost hope were sleeping off last night in doorways filled with trash, their limp hands still wrapped around paper sacks from which brown bottles protruded. I hurried up a bit.

Then I saw a "dude" approaching me. One pant leg was rolled to his knee. His shoes were not acquainted with each other; his socks were also strangers to each other. A multicolored coat swung back to reveal a gold watch chain draped to his knee. A broad-brimmed hat shaded his young face, but I thought I saw a threatening glare. He was a stranger and I was in a part of the city where drug-dealing was a daily event.

Fear seized my heart and encouraged my legs to break into a jog. I would move on quickly and with authority, I decided. As we neared each other, I looked straight ahead to avoid eye contact. Just then my toe connected with a stone the size of a goose egg and launched it with unbelievable accuracy directly into the man's exposed shin.

He doubled over, wincing in pain. And I reacted. I ran to him, grabbed his arms with both my hands, practically hugging him, and said, "Are you OK? I'm so sorry!" As his wave of pain passed, I looked into two of the kindliest eyes you'd ever want to see. He smiled. "Yeah, I'm OK. It just stung for a minute."

In seconds the event had passed. We both continued on our ways. But I still remember how fear would have created an enemy for me. Pain accidentally inflicted made us friends for a moment, though we may never meet again. Fear started in my mind and moved to my heart and my feet. The Spirit's gift of compassion conquered my fear.

We cannot deny that we live in a world dappled with dangerous spots. Teens rub each other out in gang fights. Families are rent for lack of love to bind them together. Our world needs dramatic reconstruction.

Friendship With the Lord

Francis was challenged to rebuild not only the Church but also every relationship of his life. One cannot be done without the other. Francis' conversion altered all his affiliations.

Initially, he exchanged a life of companionship for aloneness. But from that moment he was never really alone: He had the Lord. Therefore, no one was a stranger. Each person bore the potential of becoming a treasured friend. One by one he rebuilt his friendships, basing them on the knowledge that God lives in each one of us. Francis approached everyone with love. Because of one temporarily friendless man, the world has been graced by uncounted thousands who have been or will become friends in Christ through Francis.

Church and community are built on friendship with the Lord and with each other. This was made clear to me one Sunday at Mass. Sitting farther back in church than usual, I could not discern the facial features of Jesus on the crucifix. Wanting to see him more clearly, I gazed more intently, but a shadow fell across his face, making it impossible. Then I happened to glance to my left. A young mother was gazing at the infant cradled in her arms. I looked to my right and saw a weathered, wrinkled face wreathed in snowy hair. I still couldn't see the face of Jesus, but I saw his beautiful face reflected in his people.

CHAPTER FOUR

Poverty as Detachment

THE STONE WALLS of his little cell left Francis with no view save his imagination. He remembered the sound of the key as his father locked him in the cold, tomb-like room. It seemed he could still hear the echo of his father's step as he walked away to leave on yet another business trip. The gist of his departing words had been, "When I return, I trust you'll have your right mind again."

In his mind's eye, Francis recalled a happier time with his father. Then Pietro Bernardone had smiled with pride as Francis held the new garment up to the light that filtered through the narrow windows of his father's shop. The sun glinted off the gold, red and blue design of the elegant fabric. In this suit Francis would become his heart's desire—a troubadour! On their travels father and son had once met a troubadour dressed in lively garb (though not as bright and brash as this garment). He had sung for them songs of knights and kings and conquering. After that, Francis often created and sang his own refrains as he rode along.

His image of himself as a troubadour finally prompted Francis to ask his father to have a troubadour's outfit made for him. Pietro Bernardone was delighted to splurge on his son's fanciful whim. The tailor's nimble fingers had created a truly amazing garment—and an expensive one. Now when Francis sang, people would know who he was—a troubadour and Pietro Bernardone's son! The exuberant gift-giver thumped his son on the back. "Francis, you need never be concerned where your life will lead. You will always be free from worry. You have all the security and comforts of a Bernardone!"

The memory made Francis smile, a feeble turn of the corner of his mouth. Now here he was, imprisoned in a tiny closet because he wished to be free of the kind of security and comfort his father's life promised to provide. Ever since he had met that glorious woman, Lady Poverty, in a dream, material possessions had become encumbrances to be shed like the chrysalis an emerging butterfly must leave before it can soar. He was but a worm, yet God would transform him. He did not need fancy clothes to sing the songs of praise he longed to offer God. His poor old tunic worked much better for God's singer—no seams to bind arms raised in praise, no concern about fine fabric getting soiled when he fell to his knees in prayer.

But his father claimed that he knew what was best for his son—discipline. "Lock him up until he sees things my way!" But Francis never did see things his father's way again. He was released from imprisonment by Lady Pica who, with a mother's love, set him free to follow his own way, God's way for him.

In *The Challenge of Tomorrow*, historian Arnold Toynbee laments, "Unfortunately for the West and for the world, the West, and eventually the world as well, has chosen so far to follow the example of Saint Francis' father, instead of following the contrary example set by Saint Francis himself." A glimmer of hope still lingers in that statement. "So far" indicates that the future still offers the possibility of people choosing Francis' way of a simpler life instead of Pietro's dreams for his son.

What was faulty in Pietro's way of life? He provided more than adequately for his family. His business brought products that were needed for daily life in Assisi. He was not a thief or a scoundrel. We find no records of child abuse or wife-beating, even when Lady Pica released Francis from imprisonment. Perhaps Pietro's failure lay in his life's focus. His efforts were focused on himself. He thrived on the multiplication of material goods. Success only made him want more— more business, more prestige, more respect, more power. His goal was upward mobility; his idea of success was fortune, fame and power.

With his conversion Francis discarded fortune, fame and power, but ultimately wound up with all three in great measure. We can only imagine his treasures in heaven. He is known throughout the world. His spiritual power still affects millions.

Francis discovered a way of life focused on God. He sought a way of spiritual subtraction. Only by subtracting every lesser desire from his life could Francis focus fully on God. He began to shed the trappings of his former life. Horses and equipment required money and time for care; they must go. Fine clothing became a costume in which he hid; now he wanted to wear holiness in the streets of Assisi. A warm bed and a fine roof over his head yielded to a bed of boughs and stars overhead in God's bedroom. A diet of fine foods and wines yielded to begged morsels from others' castoffs. Even old friends who might lead him away from his journey to God must be left behind. Stripped of layers of desire that had gathered the illusion of necessity, Francis was free to focus on his God.

Francis was poor before God and in the sight of his family and community. Poverty was his chosen way. His poverty was not the abject, destructive poverty thrust on people by circumstances beyond their control. Francis chose to wed Lady Poverty, to bind his life faithfully to hers for all his days. Loving Lady Poverty was like returning to the Garden of Eden before the fall of Adam and Eve. Simplicity of life provided him with everything his heart desired, everything God had provided for his first creations—especially the presence of God. Because he *chose* poverty and focused on God, Francis discovered *holy* poverty. His choice led Francis on the path of downward mobility; he moved toward possessing less as he moved toward greater joy.

Poverty foisted on us without choice is not freeing. Such poverty imprisons its victims in pain and anger, hopelessness and despair. When physical violence or political injustice rip security from life, choice is absent. In the aftermath of inexplicable loss, victims sometimes relinquish their losses to God and thus experience healing through their choice to surrender their losses to God. For holy poverty is possible only when we *choose* to surrender ourselves and our possessions to God and for God.

Embracing Poverty

So how do we embrace poverty in contempo society? Most of us simply cannot sell the family h or cancel the lease on the apartment and go sleep in t park with the family. We have responsibilities to fulfill. Francis did not bequeath to the world just one way of following him. While he advocated total poverty for his friars and sisters, he understood that laypeople had different needs and responsibilities. As he said at the end of his life, "I have done what was mine to do. May the Lord teach you yours."

Our call to simplicity of life as laypeople does not include abandoning loved ones and responsibilities. We are instead to look at the heart of Francis' spirituality for inspiration to transform our lives within the context of family, friends, community, recreation and work. Then we can seek to follow the footsteps of Francis faithfully in shoes that fit our own feet. We will learn that it is not what we possess but who we become that brings us joy as we journey, free of excess, toward God.

We are not to be copycats, donning tattered tunics and begging for food in the streets as Francis did eight centuries ago. We do not have to live in squalor to adopt poverty as a life-style. Franciscan spirituality invites us to detach our hearts from property, possessions and sometimes certain people—anything that does not lead us closer to the Lord. Franciscan spirituality invites us to attach our hearts to the Lord.

Those who live the Franciscan charism offer a variety of ways to follow Francis. Larry and Anna Mae are affiliates of the Franciscan Sisters of Perpetual Adoration. Though they have been committed

their lives, their Franciscan
to a simpler life-style. Simplicity
ministry and sharing with others.
is a home away from home for
risoners is part of their mission.
cussion and action offer hope
tives to succumbing to despair
orld.

St. Francis Village in Crowley, Texas, was created
with the help of the Secular Franciscan Order. (Secular
Franciscans seek to live out Francis' Rule for laypeople
in the world of home and work.) Along streets whose
names ring like a litany of Franciscan saints and places
Francis knew, four hundred fifty residents rent rather
than own houses and apartments. A simple life-style
centers around community living, prayer and ministries
that stress the spiritual and corporal works of mercy.
Because of the community's charitable involvement, it
pays no taxes on property or purchases, making more
funds available to assist the needy.

While the above examples bear the name *Franciscan*,
many people follow the Franciscan way without the
name tag. Dr. Nesbitt was a college professor whose
colleagues gently chided him for continuing to live in a
modest home when he could have afforded to move up
the hill. "But then I would be less free to help others
with my time and money," he answered. His students,
hearing this message, learned that they had similar
choices to make in their future.

The Nagle family involves everyone in financial
planning. Parents and children sit down together on a
monthly budget night to apportion the family income.

Their plan includes a percentage to their Church. They set aside reasonable allowances for family fun and celebrations—birthdays, vacations, anniversaries. A college fund grows little by little. The balance is available for helping special people and worthy projects. One family policy is that money must be matched by family efforts. A conservancy group receives a check the day the family helps clean up the local riverbanks. The family serves the poor on Thursday evenings at the soup kitchen they support financially. Their twelve-year-old son says, "Sure, we could have more stuff, but this is more fun. My friends get to come along, too."

Nancy recalls the support a Franciscan community provided for her and her children during a painful time. "They let me know I was worthwhile even after my divorce. Their simple life-style enabled them to help me through my difficulties. They helped with the bills, with food till I could get on my feet," she remembers. "I try to live that way now. I drive a seventeen-year-old car. Although we have a nice income, that's not our focus. Franciscan life embraces so much. It is all-inclusive, for everyone. While it is totally Catholic, it's not alien to non-Catholics who also love Francis."

One woman jokes about the change that following Francis made in her handbag. "I used to be able to go on a weekend trip, sew up a dress or do minor surgery with the stuff I carried in my purse," she laughs. "And I always worried that someone would snatch it! Now I just tuck the necessities in my pocket and I'm ready to go. I trust God to take care of me. I feel much freer."

Francis did not declare material possessions and

money evil. He simply recognized them as insurmountable distractions for himself. Those who wish to follow his way discover this, too.

Francis' wisdom is reflected in contemporary life by a highway incident: A truck carrying valuable cargo accidentally dumped its load on the side of an interstate. Traffic immediately slowed and then stopped—because passersby were gathering the loot from the wrecked truck for themselves. Even travelers with no interest in helping themselves were delayed by the traffic jam.

Materialism and consumerism can dump a cargo of stuff on the road of our spiritual journey. Stopping to deal with it thwarts progress toward God.

Detachment From Self

Franciscan spirituality also calls us to avoid attachment to things of an immaterial nature: attitudes, plans, opinions, feelings, ideas, judgments, relationships. These attachments may represent a tenacious clinging to self. "It's easier to give up a sack of old clothes or canned goods than it is for me to relinquish some of my opinions," a friend said recently.

Pietro locked Francis in the small cell in the hope of keeping his son bound to Pietro's own concept of right. Pietro chose his own way. It doesn't seem to have been the right way.

Francis lived the truth of the adage, "I'd rather be right than have my own way." His conversion moved him from his way to the right way. He showed the way of openness to others in his visit to the sultan of Damietta. Knowing they did not share belief in the risen Christ, Francis focused on their mutual reverence for God. Francis refused to reject the sultan simply because they held radically different positions about Jesus. He approached him with the love of God in his heart. The sultan did not convert to Christianity but, when Francis departed, he had won the Muslim leader's respect. Francis' acceptance of the sultan reminds us to refuse to reject others because of appearances, possessions or political stances.

Fierce attachment to desires, ideas and judgments that we hold as right is the basis for prejudices: "My race is superior to yours." "Men (women) are more capable than women (men)." "Catholics are the only true Christians." "If you don't like sports (opera, chow mein or bagels), you're nuts!" These attachments represent attachment to self. When we are the center of our own universe, it is impossible to center on God. Self-detachment is difficult but imperative for spiritual growth. Striving for self-detachment does not leave us rag dolls, mindless and spineless. Instead, it leaves us selfless. The selfless person is free to focus on God and others in daily life.

How do we begin to relinquish attitudes, opinions, ideas that may hinder our Franciscan/Christian walk? We must first recognize them. To discover whether an attitude or viewpoint to which we cling is aiding us along our Christian journey, do some mental imaging. Try to visualize Jesus or Francis as citizens of your town. Dress them in today's clothing. Invite them to a quiet spot to discuss your dilemma. As you talk over the attitude in question with your companion, create an imaginary dialogue. Include your beliefs and what you think Jesus' or Francis' response might be.

Talking about your ideas in the presence of Jesus or Francis is like holding a mirror up to those concepts. The reflection of your idea reveals it for what it truly is. You may discover your stance on the matter is in keeping with Christian/Franciscan values. Or this process may expose attitudes that need review and reshaping.

Time to Waste

Simplicity and sacrifice offer the riches to be derived from poverty. Purchasing, maintaining and protecting possessions consume a large portion of daily effort. One man lamented, "I could have played a lot of games with my kids, taken long walks with my wife and fed a lot of hungry people at the soup kitchen downtown in the time I spent learning to program my VCR." He acknowledged loss of rich opportunities in life caused by one so-called modern convenience. Surveying our homes, we might calculate how many work hours were required to purchase things that we rarely use or could easily do without. For many families, extra expenditures necessitate a second income. The additional work hours rob us of leisure or family time, time to be alone and time to be at peace.

As this pattern of life escalates, being busy becomes a part of our identity. We feel unimportant if we are not doing something productive. Over the years I have accumulated a variety of "time savers"—blender, food processor, small electric chopper. I have also discovered it takes longer to clean these gadgets when I use them or when they just sit on the kitchen counter than it takes to perform tasks with them. A good, sharp knife does the job efficiently, can be quickly wiped clean and stored after use. Simplicity saves time as well as money. Time redeemed enriches our lives.

An old cliche states that we cannot buy time. True, each day contains 1,440 minutes, each year, about 8,760 hours. We cannot purchase any more than the given allotment. We can gain the use of additional minutes and hours if we have fewer excess possessions to care for, fewer valuables to guard.

What can we do with time saved by simplifying our lives? Waste it! Francis was an expert in wasting time. With no watch, no clock, far from the sound of the town's bells, Francis was not fettered by time. Since he no longer owned a horse, he walked. Sometimes he had a particular place to go; other times he simply wandered with no special destination in mind. Walking took longer but blessed him with the best of times. He could see the blossoms of the wildflowers at the roadside much better than he had from astride his horse. Traveling closer to the ground, he could bend to smell their fragrance. Sometimes he found himself nose to nose with a bee as they shared the same flower.

And then there were the children. When Francis was astride his horse, they had moved away from the flying hooves when he came galloping by like the wind. Now they scampered up to him. The brave ones grasped his hand. The timid ones smiled dusty grins. Perhaps the children were the first to sense a saint was in their midst. How did they know? He had time for them—time to waste, time to laugh and skip along the road. One day when a group of children encountered

Francis, one began to sing a child's simple song. Another pretended to play a shepherd's pipe. Yet another banged a cadence on an invisible drum. Francis, not to be left out, picked up a stick and began to play as merry a tune on his imaginary fiddle as anyone could wish. The little band marched along the dusty road playing and singing until they fell laughing in a field of hay.

When Francis realized that they had crushed some wheat in their folly, he stooped to straighten the bent stalks. The children imitated him, not wishing to cause the farmer a loss of crops.

Francis could waste time so profitably! And he found God in doing so. His Lord had said, "Let the little children come to me." Francis thought this was a great idea and followed Jesus' example.

And when their playing was done, Francis took the joy he had gathered in his heart and went off to care for people with leprosy. The hands that had held the fiddle cleansed wounds and prepared a pot of soup to nourish the emaciated bodies. Before Francis left, he passed along the smiles the children had given him to those upon whom few smiles fell.

God can find us in the leisure of our day if we share time with him in prayer or meditation. Loved ones can rediscover us in quiet moments too. Take time. It's hard to love in a hurry.

Young Timmy, talking with his dad, suddenly ordered, "Come down here, Dad!"

His surprised dad said, "But I'm right here, Timmy."

"No, you're not. You're big so you're way up there

and I have to talk to your pockets. I want to talk to your eyes!"

Dad immediately stopped his work in the garage and sat on a box where he and Timmy could talk—eye to eye. The work ceased, but love between father and son grew. It takes time to love another person. It takes time to love oneself. It takes time to love God.

CHAPTER FIVE

Living the Gospel

JUSTIN CARISIO IS, among many other things, a
Secular Franciscan and the leader of a Cub Scout
troop. He tells this story:

> Cub Scouts have a big event each year called the Pine
> Wood Derby. Each boy gets a little kit that contains a
> piece of pine, some wheels and pins from which to
> fashion a miniature race car. The night when the cars
> race down a long wooden track is very exciting,
> usually the highlight of the year.
>
> I announced the date for the race. The next day I
> received a call from a den mother who had been
> called by the mother of one of the boys in her den.
> Donny had gone home from the meeting crying
> inconsolably. He was to be admitted to the hospital
> the week of the Pine Wood Derby. I did not know that
> Donny had leukemia. His last hope was a bone
> marrow transplant. Was there any way we could
> change the date?
>
> I am not the kind of person who likes to do
> planning, nor do I like making phone calls. But I said
> I would try. I immediately called another father to see
> if we could reserve the track for a week earlier. An
> hour or two later he called back: We had it! I called
> the den leader and said, "Tell Donny's mother that

we've moved the race up. No one needs to know why."

Of course, many knew why. And the night of the race, there was Donny. All of us remember that there seemed to be magic in the air; the Spirit was among us. People kept coming up to Donny to pat his shoulder, to say something, anything. I saw then with certainty that in the context of our parish, our Cub Scout pack had become a community within a community. We were giving our collective blessing to Donny.

The den leader said, "It would be nice if Donny won something."

I replied, "I can change dates but I don't fix races." I didn't have to. Donny's car won one heat, then another and another. The end of the story is that Donny won the pack championship. He was overjoyed.

But that is not really the end of the story. Donny went to the hospital. Two months later, he died.

At the funeral home, family after family from the Cub Scout group lined up to speak to Donny's family. Along the wall were pictures of Donny in happy times. Right next to his coffin was a little table. On it, dwarfed by huge bouquets of flowers, were two things: his race car and his Cub Scout hat. I realized that winning the Pine Wood Derby was perhaps his greatest achievement of his short ten years. That is what he carried into eternity.

And I thought, "My God, my God, I could so easily have said no. I could have been too tired or too busy or too preoccupied with formalities, too stuck to the schedule. All the years I had given to Scouts may have been simply so that on that one night I would be where God wanted someone who could be counted

on to say yes out of love and compassion. He had in
that place a sojourner who realizes that we are all
here only for a moment, and that our work is not to
organize, plan and make schedules. The work of
Christian sojourners is to build the Kingdom.
Wherever we are, we must be open to the Holy Spirit
and create communities in which Christ is present.
Tomorrow we may be gone; tomorrow Christ may
come."

Justin Carisio, on a night when he was tired and would
have rather done something else, was asked to change a
date for a little boy. He said yes. In that moment he
applied the gospel to his life in an act of love and
compassion. It was only a little act—as are most acts of
life. He did nothing outrageously heroic or life-risking.
Justin did not even ramble through a mental checklist
to decide whether or not he would attempt to change
the date of the Pine Wood Derby. He simply said yes.

Francis often acted in a similar way. It is said of him
that he acted first and then attempted to figure out
why he had done what he did. That might be called
impulsiveness; in Francis it was a response that
sprang from a life steeped in gospel values. He
simply responded to those values. Bringing the
gospel to life and life to the gospel is no big deal. It is
a multitude of small deals. Each yes we say allows
the gospel to transform us.

Seek the Truth

Some decisions in life require more lengthy
discernment. Father Tom Speier, O.F.M., who leads the
Franciscan Spiritual Direction Program, offers four

simple criteria for discerning Franciscan direction in life: (1) Do you think it best to do the action in question? (2) Will the action please God? (3) Does the action follow God's plan according to the gospel? (4) Does the decision flow from a spirit of poverty? If the response to these questions is yes, proceed in your chosen direction with God's blessing and in Franciscan obedience.

Francis may not have pondered these specific points as he contemplated life's decisions, but they are clearly the guidelines of his decisionmaking as he went about rebuilding the Church. Justin Carisio also remembered that the work of Christian sojourners is to build the Kingdom here and now. That concept is explicit in the above criteria. Each yes ultimately produces a building block in the creation of the Kingdom in our midst now.

Jesus said to seek the truth and the truth will set us free (see John 8:31-32). As we attempt to live the gospel in daily life, we must also seek the truth about ourselves. That experience can be humbling. But only when we know ourselves can we be free to hear God.

Certain factors keep us from accepting the truth about ourselves. We might prefer to blame others for negative circumstances in our lives. We may fear the cost of change if we acknowledge that something is out of kilter. Such factors are filters through which we screen life's events and decisions. Filters permit us to hear only what we want to hear, only in the way we want to hear it. They screen out what may be painful to us or what may challenge us to change.

Once when the water was not flowing freely from

my kitchen faucet, I unscrewed the small filter that covers the outlet and discovered a quantity of small gravelly bits impeding the flow. When the filter was cleaned, the water once again flowed freely. Filters catch bits and pieces of our struggles in life. If we do not deal with them, they accumulate. They prevent the gospel from flowing freely in our lives. Do we filter what we disagree with through fits of anger or rage? Does compulsive or obsessive behavior separate us from gospel living? An excessive need to be accepted or to criticize others places filters in relationships. Amazing courage is required to face and cleanse the filters within us.

Reading Scripture may reveal our filters to us. If a Scripture passage makes you feel uncomfortable, reread it. Insert your own name in an appropriate place in the reading so that the message speaks directly to you. Talk to the Lord about how the passage affects you. Search within yourself to understand why you resist the message with which you struggle. Ask God in prayer why the passage raises opposition within you.

"But I say to you that listen, Love your enemies, do good to those who hate you, bless those who curse you, pray for those who abuse you" (Luke 6:27-28). As Mike heard these words, he felt himself resisting them. His hands closed, almost making fists. His jaw tightened and the muscles across his shoulders tensed. Because Mike was intent on allowing the gospel to move into his life, he read the verses several times. It seemed that God began to speak to him through them. A couple of years earlier Mike had helped a friend get a job with the company he worked for. The friend had just received a promotion—at Mike's expense. The new assignment might have been Mike's except for some misinformation his friend had dropped in important ears. Mike had not had an opportunity to defend himself in the matter. He had felt resentment toward his friend since hearing of the deception.

The Scripture brought Mike new knowledge of himself. His resentment was a filter which was keeping the gospel from his life. He began to make plans to change his way of dealing with the matter. Mike was following Francis, who took Christ's words at face value and obeyed the Lord's every command as he endeavored to bring the gospel to life, life to the gospel.

Mike needed to be free of resentment in order to respond with Franciscan attitudes and values to the circumstances of his life. He did not respond as a medieval Francis, but as a modern man rediscovering basic values in the work world.

Each stone in a stream alters the direction of the water's flow. Major stepping stones marked the ebb and flow of Francis' life. His dream of Lady Poverty initiated the realization that wealth, power and fame were not what he was called to achieve. They represented empty promises that held no prospect of peace. Francis surrendered material possessions as he gave his armor to a poor knight and his clothing to his father in the presence of the bishop. These actions revealed his choice to become vulnerable. His exterior protection was gone.

Embracing the man with leprosy was a stepping stone. Having breached his repugnance at the disease, Francis could now lovingly accept all people. Freed of superficial goals and goods, filled with love and admittedly vulnerable, Francis would undertake a fearless self-searching to discover whatever inhibited his search for God. His life plunged into prayer.

One has to live in a hermit's hut hundreds of miles from civilization to ignore the fact that something is wrong in the world today. In some this knowledge breeds despair. Young couples refuse to bring children into a troubled world. Cynicism plagues some people; depression haunts others.

The world and all its troubles have always been with us. As world population burgeons, the potential for conflict increases proportionately. Our situation appears more complex because of the vast network of communications media. We are made painfully aware of the devastation caused by each war, disaster, slaughter or uprising in the world. Newspapers carry photos of the devastation wrought by disease or drought. Earthquakes, floods, hurricanes, tornadoes and avalanches are regular fare on the nightly news. As our minds absorb this rush of information, courage may wilt. Where is God in the midst of such chaos? How can one live a gospel life in the crises of these times?

The gospel is no stranger to uncertainty and difficulty. Jesus lived in times of tumultuous political unrest. Many of his Jewish contemporaries hailed him as the one who would bring them peace through freedom from Roman rule. Animosity raged against the disciples who carried his message into the world. Francis' lifetime was marked by constant wars among lords of small states. Invaders pillaged Europe. Disease and death demanded their toll. Against a backdrop of fear, pain and death, the Good News comes to life!

Allowing the gospel to live in our lives requires sacrifice. David Purvis, a platoon leader in charge of the most northerly outpost in South Vietnam near the demilitarized zone, was acquainted with killing. During his Vietnam stint he also became acquainted with a Catholic chaplain who encouraged him to explore the truths of the Catholic faith. David became a Catholic. Some years after his conversion to Catholicism, he read of a folk singer who had become a Catholic and Secular Franciscan in response to the life-style he observed Franciscans living. The singer's choice inspired David to explore the spirituality of Saint Francis of Assisi. He began formation as a Secular Franciscan, someone who lives in the world according to the way of Saint Francis.

Purvis was by then a major in the Marine Reserves, and Reserves were on alert to intervene in trouble spots around the world. A Marine general suggested that Davis read *The Vicar of Christ*, by Walter Murphy. David read the book and began to correspond with the author. Contemplating the choices he faced, David decided, "I couldn't kill again—not for any reason. So I resigned. I was just three years short of my twenty-year pension, but I really couldn't do anything else." David continues his commitment to peacemaking. His sacrifice gives him a sense of peace.

Another military man, Richard Gain, also a Secular Franciscan, views his position in a different way. Gain's work in the United States Army involves distribution and management of supplies and materials. He sees his work as a part of the peace process, helping people in disaster areas and cooling potential hot spots. David and Richard both focus their lives on the gospel. The manner in which people achieve this in daily realities is as varied as the individuals who make choices to follow Francis.

Perhaps the gospel can only come alive in our lives when we realize that salvation means we are saved from something. Maybe that is why a sense of poverty is so essential to the spiritual life. This life will have its difficulties and then it will end. Detachment from all that would camouflage this reality is essential. Excessive pleasure-seeking, consumerism, abuse of alcohol, drugs or food are all human attempts to dodge life's realities. When we understand that this lifetime is but a speck on the eternal time line, we begin to attend to the real business of living the gospel. We live for what will last forever rather than for what is temporary.

Francis lived his vision of poverty and peace in a culture that could neither comprehend nor understand his quest. He was first mocked and ridiculed, only later revered as a saint. When we choose to live the gospel in today's culture, we can expect mockery and scorn. When we share derision and persecution for applying gospel values to everyday situations, we are sharing in the suffering of Christ and of Francis, who also met adversity as they attempted to live in a world that had forgotten to place God's values first. Tenaciously applying the gospel to today's life-style may also make us saints.

Tom Geiger entered the seminary, but decided his call was to life as a layman. In fact, he could not wait to complete seminary training; he was too anxious to work among the poor. Tom ran a soup kitchen in the inner city. He cooked. He served. He cleaned up. His efforts attracted volunteers who assisted. His place was more than a soup kitchen. It became a place where people who had lost hope could rediscover themselves and their God. After lunch was served and cleanup completed, Tom would sit and talk with those who lingered. They might play a few hands of cards and discuss life—good times and bad—and jobs—those they had had and those they could not get.

In winter Tom could be seen lugging rolls of plastic from apartment to apartment. He stapled it over drafty windows in the aging buildings. Soup kitchen volunteers would notice that Tom did not have a coat so they would bring him one. By the next week Tom would be out in the cold with no coat. He always found someone colder—needier—than he.

When his day's work was done, Tom coached high school wrestling. The boys loved him. He demanded the best from them. He went through conditioning programs with them—running, lifting weights. Then one day Tom stopped running—stopped dead in his tracks. He was only in his thirties, but his work on earth was done.

Tom died, but his goodness to the poor lives on. The Tom Geiger House in Cincinnati, Ohio, was established in an unused Catholic elementary school. A corps of volunteers did the rehabbing, supported by donations from many others. Women and their children find temporary homes in apartments created from former classrooms. While they stay, the women receive education and job training and the children experience a safe haven.

Tom could have looked at the rundown part of his city as beyond hope; instead he saw the potential for saving grace. He could have judged the residents lazy or shiftless; instead he saw God's children, his brothers and sisters. Tom Geiger lived the spirit of Franciscan life. He shunned material gifts for himself. He loved the poor. His life was a prayer of love in action. He took the gospel he knew and loved and hauled it through city streets in a roll of plastic. He stirred it into kettles of soup. He handed it over the counter in a sandwich.

The gospel is very portable. It can readily be transported anywhere in life if we are willing to become gospel-bearers. It isn't a heavy burden to bear. We don't strain to carry it on our backs. We carry it in our hearts. Christian living is like a sponge. We must soak up the gospel until we are saturated and it pours forth through our lives.

Saint Francis of Assisi did all that he did for the love of God. The only reason to fast, give alms, do acts of kindness or pray is for the love of God. It is silly to worry who will or will not see us, to be concerned if we look good or foolish, pious or proud. A good test for our motivation is: "Would I still do this if no one were watching?"

CHAPTER SIX

Peace

PEACE—MY GOD, do we want peace! So did Francis. He wanted it so much he went to war for it, fired by dreams of knighthood and glory. But along the way to becoming a warrior, Francis heard God speak to him, "Whom do you wish to serve, the Master or the servant?"

With that question echoing in his mind, Francis wheeled his horse around and began a humbling journey homeward. Of course, he wanted to serve the Master. He retreated from a war with an enemy "out there" and ventured to take on the enemy within himself. Along the way he swapped steeds and armor with a poor knight. He was beginning to understand that poverty as detachment from material property was a prerequisite to peace. Wars are fought over what people cling to—territory, treasures, traditions. Wars are not waged over what people choose to sacrifice.

I remember looking into the face of a young Rwandan priest who was doing graduate studies in Rome in 1995. One cannot imagine a more serene person. Peace radiated from his gentle eyes. His skin, dark and smooth, clothed him in innocence. His mouth seemed ready to speak soothing words of kindness.

Had he been a woman, the aura of his bearing would have made him an ideal model for a black Madonna.

Knowing his history, his face and peaceful presence were astonishing. Only weeks earlier this young man had lost every single member of his family and extended family in the tribal rivalry and slaughter in his homeland. He had grieved deeply. Now he was at peace with God. Someone asked if he would remain a priest in the aftermath of such tragedy. He replied, "Of course, of course! Now I have only God to serve." His face returns to me again and again, yet I might not recognize him if we were to meet again. His look of peace, not his features, is what is etched in memory. The beauty of his peace transcends the horror of his history. He has already experienced a resurrection. Those who meet him witness it. Returning to Rwanda, he will bear that peace with him.

This young man took the most violent type of hatred and absorbed it into his being. Relying on the amazing source of grace God offers all of us, he forgave the violators of his family, his heritage and his land. He put the hatred and violence to rest. What remains in him is peace. He is a source of awe to all who meet him. His witness to the peace that passes all human understanding flows out into the world in rippling circles. People like "Father Rwanda," as I've come to call him, can change the world.

When the evening news comes on, acts of senseless violence—is there any other kind?—first cause anger and sadness to rage within me. Then I remember Father Rwanda. What can we do about such tragedy, which seems beyond our power to erase? We can pray for both perpetrators and victims. Because I think and pray in images, I visualize the two sides coming together with each other in the healing presence of Jesus.

In prayer I try to be like the courageous soldier my dad told about after World War II. During training a frightened GI dropped the grenade he was about to throw. The pin had been pulled. Without hesitation another soldier threw himself on the rolling grenade. Had it not been for his courage, I might have grown up without Dad. The soldier gave his life, wrapping himself around potential evil so that others might live.

In prayer we can wrap our spirits around those who do not know the gospel way of life. We can absorb some of the hatred simply by refusing to pass it along through our own hostility. Perhaps these prayer techniques do not change the chemistry between victims and violators. They may. I am quite certain, however, that I am changed by viewing those in conflict in this manner. Seeing the Lord in the midst of those who would create havoc is a reminder that with God all things are possible.

'God Loves You!'

Not all actions for peace are heroic. For Francis, peace was simply having no enemies. Francis would allow no one to rob him of his peace by becoming his enemy. One who succeeds in stealing our peace becomes an enemy.

Once a woman had her purse snatched on the street. Before the thief could run away, the woman grabbed him and demanded, "Give it back so I can give it to you!" The astonished man handed the purse to her.

The woman reached inside, took out her money and, true to her word, gave it to the man. "Now you won't be guilty of stealing from me," she told him. The abashed would-be thief looked at the money and the woman, then handed the money back and went on his way. The woman had refused to allow the man to become her enemy. She would not be his enemy either. Peace is having no enemies. Peace is following Francis.

I imagined Francis watching the evening news with us recently. Scenes of carnage in civil war blotched the international scene. Nearer home, kids with guns stained the streets with other children's blood. I speculated about what Francis would do if faced with such tragedy.

In my imagination he leaped from the couch, intent on walking to the part of the city where children warred with one another over drugs or turf. With a bit of convincing, he reluctantly allowed us to drive him to that troubled part of town. When we arrived, he threw open the car door, jumped out and began to dance and sing among the harbingers of hatred, "God loves you! God loves you! Love one another! God loves you!" In the hot summer night, some kids standing on the corners scoffed. Others laughed, then began to join in the dance and the chant. "God loves you!" The crowd grew. Even the scoffers were drawn into the joyful gathering.

Then Francis said, "But we must move on. There are other parts of town where folks don't know God's love." So we drove to a neighborhood of manicured lawns and stately architecture. No throngs crowded the street in the quiet evening. Francis began to sing again,

"God loves you! God loves you!" After a few minutes a face appeared from behind a closed window blind to stare at the strange goings-on. Francis knocked on the door, but no one would answer. He scampered to the house next door. There his knock was answered. The door opened as far as the security chain would permit. "God loves you!" Francis reminded the inhabitant. "We go to church," a timid voice said. The door closed. Across the street a family emerged from their house. "God loves you, too!" The dad called, "Come on over. Have a glass of iced tea. Let's talk."

Peace is impossible without the knowledge that God loves us. Peace is within reach with the realization that we are beloved of God. God is love and with God all things are possible. Many hear the good news of God's love. Their responses are diverse.

My husband, son and I watched a couple take their seats in the first row at a major league baseball game. As they entered, they made every attempt to attract attention. Their dress and behavior made one wonder if they loved themselves. They blocked the view of those behind them as they stood for every play. A snowy-haired grandmother-type seated behind them could not see the plays. "Down in front!" spectators yelled. Often the pair turned to the crowd, chastising others for not cheering as loudly as they yelled. When they faced the playing field, you could read the man's T-shirt, which commanded, "Shut Up and Drink Your Beer!" Through several innings people endured the disruption, but negative comments abounded, "Jerks!" "Have you ever seen any like 'em?" The body language of others around them revealed disgust at their behavior.

Earlier, a father had wheeled a child who had cerebral palsy to their seats. He carried the heavy child to his seat, situated him on a cushion, then took the wheelchair where it would be stored until the game's end. His efforts were clearly a labor of love. Then they proceeded to have a wonderful time enjoying the ball game.

As the game progressed, a player known for his rapport with the crowd came near the fence where the noisy couple sat. He tossed a baseball to a child waving her glove in the air. As he tossed another, the long arm of the man in the "Shut Up" T-shirt snagged it. Another went to a happy child's hand. A few minutes later the disruptive woman also grabbed a ball tossed to the kids. By this time the spectators surrounding the couple were aggravated. Why had these disorderly people gotten two balls when little kids were walking away empty-handed?!

Looking at the boy with cerebral palsy, my husband commented, "You know, those two could make that boy's day if they shared one of those balls with him."

"Why don't you ask them?" I ventured.

"What good would it do?" he answered without a hint of hope. "No way!" was our son's response to the same invitation.

An usher came down the aisle. Half joking, my husband pointed out the boy and the couple and asked that the usher make the suggestion.

"You gotta be kidding!" he replied. "That guy'd probably punch me out! They were jerks when they came in and they'll be jerks when they leave!" I was struggling with my own feelings about the hostility that surrounded these people—especially my own attitude, which mentally echoed the "Jerks!" spoken by more than one person. These people were becoming my enemies although I did not even know them. The collective judgment of the crowd left little room for charitable acts on their part.

"What would Francis do if he were here?" my mind asked. Suddenly, as if Francis himself lifted me from my seat, I found myself walking down the aisle toward the couple. I could hear our son say, "Oh my gosh, there goes Mom!" Bending down, I told the two about the handicapped boy, suggesting that they could make him a happy guy by sharing one of the balls. The man clutched the ball he had retrieved as if he thought I might snatch it from him. But without hesitation the woman said, "I can do that!" She rose from her seat with a big smile on her face and went to the boy to offer him the ball.

What happened among that gathering of baseball fans was fascinating. The couple's disruptive behavior stopped. The man and woman sat in their seats, cheering enthusiastically at appropriate times. They smiled at each other and gave each other a couple of arm-around-the-shoulder hugs. Watching the people who had been irritated by the two, one could observe a decided change in attitude. Hostility vanished. Those who had seen the woman offering the ball gestured toward her with smiles of appreciation as they explained to their companions what had transpired.

Other acts of kindness followed. A young girl who was watching her first major league game offered the ball she had caught to my husband. She had heard him say he had come to the ballpark for twenty-five years and never caught a ball. He refused, of course, but her offer was a precious gift.

Even though our team lost the game, this group of fans went home winners. The couple did not go home jerks, as the usher had prophesied. The woman's gesture of loving-kindness altered many people's attitudes. Peacemaking can come wrapped in the tiniest of endeavors inspired by the Franciscan way of having no enemies.

CHAPTER SEVEN

Reverence for Creation

WHEN I WAS A SMALL CHILD, I discovered two interesting brownish orbs on a flower stem in Grandma's garden. Not knowing what they were, I plucked the stem and took the papery objects into the house. Grandma explained that they were praying mantis nests. Then I laid them down—in a room that was just the right temperature at just the right time for them to hatch! One of God's miracles must be the number of infant praying mantises packed into a one-inch featherweight tan sphere. Millions? Zillions? When Grandma and I returned to the room later, the walls were crawling with the tiny creatures.

Did Grandma hand me a broom while grabbing a can of insecticide to use herself? Of course not! She got a dustpan and a sheet of paper. She gently slid the paper under the batches of praying mantis babies adorning her walls. Then she dumped them from the paper into the dustpan. I carried the pan outside to set the minuscule captives free. The operation took quite a long time. As we worked, Grandma explained the value of these small creatures to her garden and to the world and why we must be careful not to harm them. The message was very strong that all God's creatures have value (though as a dog owner I have some serious doubts about fleas!).

The hour or so spent debugging Grandma's house left a profound impression on me that will last a lifetime. All of God's creation is of value, though sometimes the link between a particular critter's value and us may be obscure. Time and effort are required to care for creation. Protecting creation may result in reduced profits in business endeavors. Still, each creature and every element of God's created earth deserve respect. In revering God's creation, we give honor and glory to God.

Francis realized centuries ago the value of the tiniest member of God's created family. He revealed it in everyday actions. Francis' days of total rejection by the residents of the town of Assisi were past. The children no longer hurled stones at him. Mothers turned to their kitchens for scraps of food when they saw him at the door rather than chasing him with a broom. Fathers still feared their sons might follow him, but secretly they admired his ability to live such a simple life.

This is a story of how Francis might have treated one of God's most insignificant creations. One warm summer day the sun caused Francis to have a great thirst. Not as great as his consuming thirst for God, of course, but one that had to be slaked. He was parched. Francis walked to the fountain in the Piazza del Comune to drink from its flowing waters. As he walked to the fountain, he looked down at the large stones slicked by the feet of countless humans and animals. Francis was amazed to see a small worm writhing on the skillet-hot surface. The small creature was desperately attempting to make its way to a cooler spot in the soft earth. But there was no earth to be found nearby. Even the cracks between the paving stones were hard and impenetrable. As he reached down, Francis wondered how the worm had gotten so far from a safe place. Perhaps it had fallen from a passing cart or from a basket of flowers or vegetables picked from the gardens below the town.

Gently scooping the wriggling worm into the palm of his hand, Francis turned from the fountain to carry the worm to safety. He looked at a small clump of grass near the door of a house. That might do for a short time, but surely the worm would venture back into the traffic of the street if it were left in the grass. A window box of blossoms and earth offered another option but, pondered Francis, "What if Brother Worm crawled over the edge and plummeted to the street once again?" Francis determined that his small friend would be safe on the land outside the walls of Assisi.

Disregarding his own thirst, Francis cupped the worm in his hand as he walked, almost running, through the crooked streets, down winding stairs to the city gate. Once outside, he walked away from the traveled road. He found a large leafy plant that provided shade for the surrounding earth. There he placed the little representative of all of God's creation and bade him farewell, saying, "*Addio*, Brother Worm; be cautious where you venture. The ways of the world can be harsh for tiny ones such as you."

Francis knew the words of the psalm Jesus quoted from the cross: "I am a worm, and not human" (Psalm

22:6a). Those words echoed in his heart as he returned to the city gate. Knowing all of creation is linked together, Francis humbly thanked God for permitting him to bring salvation—at least for a while—to a worm, one to whom Jesus compared himself.

Francis was a man of extremes. His drastic approach to sometimes minor situations serves to alert us to the way life's greater values are revealed in small ways. In striving to be poor, he discarded all possessions. In grasping for peace in a warrior world, he refused to harm even a worm. Francis' actions teach that if we reverence even the smallest works of art in God's creation, we will not desecrate the more significant ones. If we respect a worm, can we choose to harm a human? Kindness to the littlest creatures is the building block for protection of all creation.

But what of the farmers or gardeners who depend upon their crops for a livelihood or yield for their family? What are they to do with the worm that devours their fruits, vegetables and flowers? The dominion God granted humans over the land is a responsibility to be carried out with the least possible destruction to creation. After a few decades of using heavy chemicals to control pests and increase crop production, some agricultural experts now discover that old techniques of fertilization and crop rotation combined with natural pest control actually enhance harvests.

Dominion indicates sovereignty over creation. The most effective sovereignty in political terms is a benevolent relationship with those who are ruled. The same applies to utilizing the resources of the earth. We cannot salvage each and every worm on the berm or toad on the road or loon on the lagoon, but Francis does call us to rule our terrain with kindness.

As a "city girl," Mary Lou has not always found God's natural creation inviting. In fact, while on a southern vacation, she saw a salamander inching his way down a palm tree, menacingly, right toward her. Birds waiting for crumbs to drop from her plate provided a feathery threat at her feet. She contemplated ending the sojourn in the south because of the wildlife until the opening phrase of Genesis—"In the beginning"—entered her thoughts. Then she began to view creation from a new perspective—as part of God's plan, a plan that was good.

Her newfound reverence for the creepy-crawly creatures of God's creation led her to new adventures in gardening. Marigolds and cucumbers, daisies and corn, tomatoes and peppers mingle with the inevitable bugs and other crawling creatures in her garden. Mary Lou believes her newfound creative activity helps her express what she feels in her soul. In the beginning God saw goodness in everything. We are called to discover the same about creation and about ourselves.

The creative powers of individuals are God-given gifts. Youths who learn to revere the beauty of their own creative abilities through art, dance, music or writing will find satisfaction in those endeavors. Secure in their own self-worth, they will be less inclined to harm others. Creativity defuses the desire to destroy. The choir director who raises a chorus of superb children's voices in the inner city helps set the children free to become the people God has created them to be.

Vandalism diminished in a section of the city where teens designed and painted a mural on a wall bordering a main street.

A young man with cerebral palsy offered to perform Native American dances for a retreat group. The performance was dramatic because the boy, though he walked with gawky awkwardness, was an accomplished Indian dancer. His dancing freed him to believe he could be a contributing member of the group. He believes he can accomplish much more in life.

Underprivileged children who discover the magic of Shakespeare through the teachings of a dedicated teacher go on to uncover other mysteries of learning. Students from more affluent backgrounds are more apt to avoid the negative temptations of their culture if they find meaning in life from a theater group or young people's orchestra. A group of older women teaches young fingers to knit as the two generations share stories of their growing-up years. Mentors working one-on-one with young people empower them to see gifts within themselves that may be dimmed by the financial or emotional impoverishment of their families or the deficiency of education available to them.

As individuals discover their roles as cocreators with God of the world around them, they respond to the gentler nature of ongoing creation. Discovering a variety of creative outlets for their passions and life's energy, children will be less likely to bear babies as a form of substitute creativity; the young will be less likely to strike out against themselves and each other in their frustrations with a complex world; the old will be less inclined to despair of their value in life's latter years.

While Francis left no paintings or sculpture, he responded to his initial call from the Lord by re-creating tumbledown little churches on the hills and in the valleys around Assisi. A divine rehabber, we might call him, a spiritual architect/builder. Many biographers of Francis of Assisi have explained that Francis' rebuilding of church edifices was actually a misreading of his spiritual call. Yet, while building with stone and mortar was not God's ultimate call for Francis, the creative effort it required gave a tangible form to the course of his life. We find no evidence that Francis regretted his early activity of rebuilding dilapidated churches. It was simply an early part of God's creative plan for Francis' life. Rebuilding churches was what Francis' hands did while his heart searched for the avenue he was to travel.

Two young boys and their dad are rebuilding a tree house in the yard behind our house. On weekends I can hear the sawing and hammering. One day the rhythm of the hammer sounded like the dad was working, but when I looked out, I saw the nine-year-old wielding the hammer. The father has taught his son so well that their work resounds to the same beat. The results of the efforts of the father and his sons on the tree house also echo in the early mornings when the dad leaves for work. "Love you, Dad!" calls one young carpenter. "Love you!" Dad calls back. For this family, the tree house is not the ultimate objective, though it is a worthwhile project that is being done well and will provide much pleasure. The tree house represents a creative outlet wherein the boys learn to do as the father teaches while love grows.

The chapels Francis repaired were not the ultimate goal God intended. They symbolized Francis' journey as he learned to follow his Father. They were the creative work along the way as Francis learned to say in ever deepening ways to his Father, "I love you!"

Creativity Versus Competition

American culture prides itself on its competitive spirit. *Bigger* and *better* become passwords for improvement. Competition can indeed produce excellence. If your tennis game is to improve, you need to play with players above your present ability level. As a runner or swimmer, you may profit from working with a stronger individual, who will push you to your potential. Those who sell strive for higher sales figures. Researchers race for new discoveries. Entertainers seek larger audiences. Churches invite more to membership in their congregations.

To a certain degree competition is creative. Creating a faster runner, a more efficient product, a bigger market for goods are positive goals. In such creative endeavors everyone wins. But when crushing competition rather than spawning creativity becomes the goal, everyone loses. This occurs when it is no longer sufficient for athletes to perform at their peak, and they resort to drugs or game-fixing. It happens when the desire to succeed in business transcends established ethical standards, and people and businesses are destroyed rather than created.

A noted professor, invited to teach business ethics

to a group of MBA's at an esteemed business school, found he could not accomplish the task. He claims the graduate students were so centered on rising in their own careers that they denied the existence of moral standards and ethical behavior in order to achieve their goals. Their competitive thrust drove higher values from their thoughts. The professor also claims that, rather than serving consumers' real needs, companies prey on appetites, emotions and the subconscious of the public. Employees, too, are swept into the stream of striving to satisfy their own appetites for success.

On a contrasting note, a businessman named Ernie registered for courses leading to certification in lay pastoral ministry in his diocese. The courses altered his view of his professional work. His newfound direction and values influenced discussions at meetings he attended for his firm. The upper management of the company invited him to meet with them. The result was that Ernie was invited to teach business ethics to his fellow employees. Work and religion were no longer separate, like parallel rails on a train track. He discovered that religious life must permeate everyday activity in order to be authentic. Spiritual and religious issues form the most solid skeleton upon which business, social and family life are enfleshed.

Francis was the antithesis of competition. He constantly wanted to be less and require less so that Christ could be more in his life. Even as Francis attempted to become less so that Christ could increase in him, people flocked to him. Wisdom and holiness flowed from his being.

Humility can be overwhelmed by competition. It

can thrive when God the Creator is acknowledged as the source of creativity. Choosing the path of destructive, crushing competition leads not to an attitude of humility, a virtue, but to the sin of pride.

Multitudes follow Francis' way because it is as little and simple as Francis himself. We "succeed" in his way by becoming less. We are freed from the competitive nature of our times that insist more is better. We realize in our spirits that "more" is insatiable. The more we have the more we crave. We may scoff at the public personality who owns thousands of pairs of shoes. The challenge is to search for the insatiable areas of our own life. Creature comfort, affirmation, success, leisure can all demand ever greater levels of fulfillment, which in turn demand more and more.

"Appetudes"—attitudes toward the appetites in life—are deceptive and can become addictive. Addictions divert our attention and energy from the pain within that we are unwilling to confront. That pain invariably is a symptom of some form of alienation from God. We recognize the addictive nature of alcohol, drugs, nicotine or excessive food consumption. More subtle addictions may be relationships that turn addictive when unhealthy dependence on another locks us into the alliance.

An electric fan formerly cooled us on hot summer days. Then air-conditioning entered the scene, altering the level of creature comfort which many consider acceptable for their contentment. Of course, air-conditioning is not bad. Health concerns, security factors or architectural design make air-conditioning almost mandatory in many situations. Geographic areas that were not generally habitable in the past because of intense heat and humidity were developed following the invention of techniques for cooling air. But the insatiable nature of the invention becomes apparent when sweaters are necessary to survive the chill of an air-conditioned indoor summer. Some people acclimate their bodies and life-styles to a range of temperatures so limited that they cannot venture outside in warm weather without complaint. Cost factors—both economical and ecological—do not dissuade those for whom more becomes paramount. As we check our priorities in life, we may ask if we are more concerned about being comfortable to Christ or comfortable in the world.

As Christians following the way of Francis of Assisi, what do we want to win besides souls and heaven? Jesus has already accomplished that for us. We respond by creating in our lives attitudes and atmospheres of love and concern for all people.

CHAPTER EIGHT

Joy

JOY IS A MISUNDERSTOOD WORD. It is often confused with happiness. Francis understood the difference between the two. *The Little Flowers of St. Francis* tells how one cold, wintry day Francis and Brother Leo were walking toward St. Mary of the Angels when Francis decided to teach Leo the meaning of joy—not just ordinary joy but perfect joy.

Francis told Leo about all the admirable attributes of character and spirit that one might live by—holiness, integrity, enlightenment. Yet desirable as they might be, they do not constitute perfect joy. The two walked on in the bone-chilling winter of Umbria, their frayed tunics blowing in the wind that whipped down the mountain slope. Francis then enumerated the blessed gifts of healing—giving sight to the blind, hearing to the deaf, mobility to the lame, speech to the dumb, life to the dead. Remarkable as these gifts might be, Francis claimed they are not to be counted as perfect joy.

Growing more excited as he considered perfect joy, Francis cried to Leo that even if one possessed enormous knowledge of all languages, sciences and Scripture plus a gift of prophecy to unveil the future and the secrets of others' minds and subsconscious, perfect joy still could not be found in these amazing gifts. One might speak like an angel, trace the course of the universe and know all the mysteries of the natural world, but perfect joy would not be found in these abilities. Even if one possessed the ability to preach the Good News so that everyone in the whole wide world would be converted to Christ, perfect joy would not be found in that astonishing gift.

Leo, realizing that Francis had eliminated every aspect of life that might be considered joyful, finally begged Francis to tell him what constitutes perfect joy.

"When we arrive home, little brother, soaked with rain, miserable from the cold, muddy and hungry, and ring the bell and the brother who answers asks in anger, 'Who are you?' And we answer, 'Two of your brothers.' And he charges, 'You lie! You are rascals out to deceive and steal from the poor! Go away!' And he slams the door. If we remain until nightfall in the snow and rain without shelter or food; if without anger or complaint we think in love and humility that the brother really knows who we are but that God makes him speak against us: That, Brother Leo, is perfect joy!

"If we persist in knocking at the door and the brother chases us away with curses and blows and we patiently endure the insults with joy and love in our hearts: That is perfect joy! If we persist in our desire to enter and are met by the brother with a club and he beats us and throws us to the ground, and we bear all these evils with joy and patience: That is perfect joy!"

Then Brother Leo, his body aching at the thought of such punishment in the face of having done no wrong, heard Francis' conclusion. "The greatest gift Christ gives to his friends is that of conquering ourselves and willingly enduring insult, humiliation and hardship for Christ. We can glory in tribulation and affliction, as Saint Paul says: 'May I never boast of anything except the cross of our Lord Jesus Christ!'" (Galatians 6:14a).

Witnesses to Joy

A dear Franciscan friend, Silas Oleksinski, who is suffering from cancer, has just been taken by ambulance to the hospital. Tomorrow he was to have moved back to the city where he ministered much of his life, back to where those who love him here could be in touch with his joyful spirit. Earlier today I learned that Laura, a brilliant young art director, died from a malignant brain tumor, leaving two young sons. Another friend, Roger, lies awaiting death, also from a brain tumor. In the midst of days like this, Francis' words about joy assume a human face—the faces of Silas and Laura and Roger.

Laura believed her illness served as a catalyst for healing within her family. Brothers and sisters began to see each other in a new light as they dealt with their sister's final illness.

Roger spoke long before his illness of the joyful anticipation he felt for the beatific vision—the vision of God that would come with bodily death.

Silas refers to his illness as Sister Cancer, his therapy as Brother Radiation. When speaking of the meaning of serious illness, Silas said the lessons those who love the sick learn in the course of illness are important, but the most important lesson of life-threatening illness is becoming acquainted with one's own soul. The soul is our touch point with God. The soul is the place within our humanity when the spirit of the living God lives vibrantly, even in—perhaps especially in—those whose suffering opens their souls to the perfect joy of God.

It is interesting to note that in the story Leo did not ask Francis *what* perfect joy was; he asked *where* perfect joy was. Perfect joy is not a thing or object. It might better be described as a place where one's spirit arrives after an arduous journey. You know how good home looks at the end of a long trip. Runners experience a euphoria in running great distances despite the fact that their bodies ache, hearts pound and lungs feel ready to burst. These are imperfect comparisons to be sure, but they hint of the joy to be anticipated when focus is unblinkingly fastened on the place where perfect joy can be experienced.

Perhaps perfect joy blooms after patients and families have knocked on God's door repeatedly with petitions for healing. Perfect joy may be unleashed in its glory when bodies are pummeled by all the life-saving therapies known to medicine only to have the illness recur. Perfect joy may be attainable only after we let go of the life we cherish—whether it be our own or that of a loved one. When we hear Francis' explanation of perfect joy to Brother Leo, we may be tempted to say, "Thank you very much. I don't care for any!" But perfect joy may be like a truffle. A truffle is an ugly fungus traditionally dug out from underground decaying matter by pigs. Its taste is exquisite. Rarity and desirability keep its price dear.

Illness is obviously not the only pathway to perfect joy. Total rejection by someone to whom you have done no wrong can lead to perfect joy when dealt with in love and acceptance. Persecution and character assassination can produce perfect joy if you avoid resentment and retribution. Loss of employment when you have committed yourself to excellent job performance can foster perfect joy if accepted as an opportunity for new challenge.

"Offer it up" is a phrase that echoes from generations past. When a trial is offered to God for whatever intention, the offer must not be retracted. It becomes God's to deal with and we become God's to be dealt with through our difficulties. God's dealings with those who are faithful in the face of adversity produce perfect joy. Franciscan author Father Leonard Foley said with enthusiasm from the moment of his diagnosis with cancer until his life drew to a painful close, "God is good and life is wonderful!" The sick, the rejected teach us what is of value in life. Through their struggles they have found the pearl of great value—perfect joy.

Perfect joy does not spawn questions like "Why me?" "Why didn't God...?" "How could you...?" Perhaps perfect joy began with Mary's response to the angel, "Let it be done to me as you say." We know the suffering that was to come from her willingness to relinquish control of her life to God. We are assured that her destiny was complete union with her Son when her earthly sufferings were complete.

A 'Place' of Joy

The place of perfect joy may seem barren—a place where nothing exists, a place where all has been relinquished, a place of total emptiness. Yet that void is the place where God can enter in perfect fullness. Perfect joy floods the place that is prepared for God.

Still, the image of a place limps. A place indicates a definite location of which one can make a map, where one can enter, perhaps close the door, mark the spot. Perfect joy cannot be confined by the concept of place. Perfect joy may best be described as a state of being at one with Christ on the cross, where the crosses of our lives have been affixed to the cross of Jesus.

Jesus no longer hangs on that instrument of torture. Because he was lifted down, because he was raised, we do not have to hang on our crosses either. We take up our crosses daily, but we do not have to hang on them helplessly. We carry them. They do not keep us nailed in one place of pain.

I once experienced perfect joy in an unlikely place, according to the world's standards. The chaplains at Children's Hospital Medical Center in Cincinnati, Ohio, plan periodic memorial services to remember the children treated at the facility who have died within the last months. A sense of overwhelming collective sorrow permeated the area where the scheduled service was to be held. As you stepped from the elevator into the hallway adjoining the room, grief smacked you in the face with all its force and pain. Families hugged each other. People who had not dared to speak to each other as they saw each other across the intensive care unit now were free to share their losses and their tears.

Amid all the emotional turmoil in the room, one couple stood out. They were considerably older than the parents who came to remember. But unlike other older people, grandparents to the deceased, this couple was all alone. They exuded a tranquility that was unique to the occasion. Sitting quietly, they shared occasional words and gentle smiles with each other while waiting for the service to begin. I went to welcome them. They shared their story. They had come to remember their child, who had recently died of cystic fibrosis in his early twenties. They also were commemorating the deaths of three of their other children, who had also succumbed to the same disease. Four children lost to the same disease—an illness that robs the young of vitality, then wrenches them from their families.

They explained that I was not to feel sorry for them. With the first diagnosis they had agonized over their child's plight. With the second they were stunned. They faced the criticism of those who challenged why they chose to have more children when the genetic possibility threatened more cases of cystic fibrosis. Intermingled with the four CF children, however, were three perfectly healthy offspring. By the time the third and fourth children were born with CF, the family had no difficulty realizing the blessedness of each child no matter what the child's physical condition. They enabled all of their children to live to the fullest potential possible. They released their children to God's care while giving them the best parental and medical care available. This couple comes close to perfect joy. It was made possible only by great suffering and deep faith.

If there is "work" to be done in achieving perfect joy, it may come from beating our swords of anger, loss and hostility into plowshares of love and peace with which to cultivate the world. The process is difficult, but all things are possible with God.

CHAPTER NINE

Prayer

WE COULD SIMPLY SAY that Francis' prayer life was, "My God and my all!" and stop at that. Everything that can be stated about prayer in the life of Saint Francis of Assisi is expressed in those five little words. While the truth is contained in that brief and holy phrase, the way in which Francis reached that apex of prayer needs exploration. In searching Francis' journey in prayer, we discover our own way to believing and living "my God and my all!" Many events in Francis' life shaped his prayer life. Among the significant markers in Francis' prayer life are four that we will explore: the crucifix, the caves, the Canticle and the stigmata.

The Crucifix

Francis is not remembered as a miracle-worker. Rather, he touched people's hearts, bringing them to Christ for transformation from within. Francis' way was empowered by his experience before the crucifix at the Church of San Damiano. His heart was changed by the words he heard there, "Go and rebuild my Church, which is falling into ruin."

In Francis' day, the Roman Catholic Church was in need of reform. Indeed, it always is. That is not an unjust criticism of the Church, but an accurate observation that any institution guided by humans, even those deeply committed to God's work, requires constant renewal. The Church is no exception. The ways of the world worm their way into God's house, causing places to sag with decay. Untended, the structure will eventually collapse.

For decades a lovely old Victorian farmhouse stood by the side of a road that our family traveled. The residents had moved away. Waist-high grasses and weeds surrounded the house. As years passed, decay set in. First windows were broken, leaving gaping holes staring at the road. Shutters drooped at odd angles, then tumbled down. Porches sagged as termites and rot undermined their supports. Then the roof caved in. One day when we drove by, the old house was gone.

I miss that old house. Its architecture was beautiful even when it was falling into ruin. But more than that, it was an ever-present reminder of Christ's instruction to Francis to rebuild his house. Any house, whether a structure or a spiritual home, must be tended in order to thrive and survive. Our spiritual houses—families, parishes, communities and nations—must be cared for by people who love them.

Francis always prayed face-to-face with the crucified Christ, whose suffering, death and resurrection provide the foundation for the Church of Francis' time and ours. Whether kneeling in front of the Byzantine cross now known as that which spoke to Francis or facing those "crucified" by the scourge of leprosy, the pain of poverty or the arrogance of affluence, Francis saw that suffering formed the foundation of faith in Christ. The face on the crucifix was the face of a suffering world.

In our day the images of bodies lying with outstretched arms on ghetto streets remind us of the crucified Christ. Children reaching out for bowls of food in famine-afflicted areas imitate the crucified Christ. People in hospital beds in hospice units represent the dying Christ. Arms grasping for a child who tumbled from a refugee truck in Bosnia suggest a type of crucifixion. If we cannot find the crucified Christ in these images, we may have difficulty finding him anywhere.

In our everyday lives we must never write off the reality of suffering: "If they would just work harder!" "They're getting what they deserve." "It's God's will!" Suffering in whatever form it assumes confronts us with the crucified Christ. God's created beings are suffering. Suffering calls for a response that begins in prayer, leads to action and returns us to prayer.

Jim Flickinger recalls his concern as he watched the events of the former Yugoslavia unfold. Those caught in the strife faced winter without fuel and proper clothing. Men, women and children confronted illness without medical supplies. Jim and his family decided to help by gathering clothes and sending them through a group linked with Bosnia-Herzegovina.

That was just a foot in the door. Later Jim and a couple of friends made contact with pharmaceutical companies, who agreed to provide medicines at a fraction of their cost. They recruited other businesses to assist with shipping the supplies overseas. Automobile manufacturers donated vans to serve as ambulances in the war-torn region. In two years Jim and his friends sent medical supplies worth more than five million dollars to the war zone.

Jim accompanied the shipments in person to assure that they reached those in need. His presence reminded the refugees that people in the outside world cared about their plight. Jim made seven trips abroad to date. "Yes," he said, "I feel a bit apprehensive before I leave. But once I'm there with the people, there's no more fear." The project, called Bright Light, Inc., never recruited funds. Benefactors simply heard the good news of the project and sent donations.[1]

Groups in the Amazon region of Brazil heard of Jim's work and sought assistance for the destitute in an area known as "Green Hell." The demise of rubber plantations left a million and a half people stranded in the tropical jungle community with no work, no vision for the future—only a decaying educational system. Leprosy plagues the population. Eight leper colonies with as many as three thousand inhabitants (including the families of the afflicted) dot the area. Leprosy is controllable with proper care and medications. Perhaps Jim's new venture can help.

Personal suffering can transform our lives, leading us to prayer, action and perfect joy. In Jim's case the suffering of others led a person with a sensitive spirit down the same road. He has responded to those being

---

[1]Bright Light, Inc., 1745 Lake Michigan Drive, N.W., Grand Rapids, MI 49504.

crucified by war, disease and ignorance. Jim Flickinger and his friends are on the verge of more perfect joy as their efforts reach from Eastern Europe to the Amazon.

We may not be able to change the situation "out there," but we can allow ourselves to be transfigured by Christ crucified again and again in the world in which we live.

This is the prayer tradition says Francis prayed before the crucifix:

Most high, glorious God,
enlighten the darkness of my heart
and give me, Lord,
a correct faith,
a certain hope,
a perfect charity, sense and knowledge,
so that I may carry out
your holy and true command.

If we choose to make this our prayer before the crucified Christ, we must digest it spiritually. We must admit that dark exists in our lives and be willing to let the light enter to illumine the dark.

"Most high, glorious God": Is God the first, most high consideration in our lives? Or does our image in our community or workplace rank above God? Is our concept of God glorious? Or is our God a vengeful God, punitive and unloving?

"Enlighten the darkness of my heart": Are we able to acknowledge the darkness in our own hearts? Denial is one of the strongest psychological blocks to changing our lives. Those suffering from addictions to food, alcohol, drugs, nicotine and unhealthy relationships rely on denial to bolster their beliefs that their addictions do not harm them or those close to them. Darkness in our hearts permits us to deny that we need to forgive others or seek their forgiveness. Darkness in our hearts allows us to project our own shortcomings on others rather than deal with them as part of our own darkness. God sent Jesus as the light of the world to enlighten our darkness.

"And give me, Lord, a correct faith, a certain hope, a perfect charity, sense and knowledge": Francis sought the gifts and fruits of the Holy Spirit to enlighten the darkness he acknowledged within himself. He did not treasure these gifts for himself, but used them for the benefit of others. Where do we turn for discernment to know whether our attitudes are correct, certain and perfect? Prayer, Scripture and spiritual companions open our minds and spirits to God's plan for us.

"So that I may carry out your holy and true command": When we are given direction, the responsibility becomes ours to carry out God's plan in our own lives.

This prayer, believed and lived, led Francis to proclaim from the depth of his soul, "My God and my all!" It promises the same results for us.

Caves

In the caves of Mount Subasio Francis plunged into prayer, seeking God while discovering himself.

> Caves in the land, they frightened me—
> gloomy, dark and deep,
> shut off from the lightened sky,

cold and damp, lonely, dank,
surrounding me in stone
like burial tombs from ages past.

Caves of myself, I loathe them most—
an open mouth of damning words,
deep chasms of my selfishness,
black holes within my soul,
voids longing to be filled,
relationships' most empty realms,
deadly pits of doubt.

Caves of the Spirit, wombs of life—
darkened dens where one can wait
when chilling fear alarms,
then face the lightened world
secure in Christ's illuminating love.

Caves in which to rest
when weary of life's tasks
allow one to reappear,
renewed in joy and in strength.

Caves like Elijah's mountain shrine,
beset by wind and fire,
where past its open face
a gentle breeze did drift uniting him with God,
still beckon me to be a gentle breeze.

Caves where Saint Francis plunged and hid,
then rose to surface
with Spirit-gifted growth,
offer sanctuary for our pilgrim feet.

Caves no longer frighten me
with darkness, damp and deep,
when I recall that in their space
God can whisper on a breeze

and call me to his light.

A friend once planned an exciting day for us—
spelunking in the rolling Indiana hills. "Sounds great!"
I said without a further thought about the adventure.
But when we arrived at the cave, what had appeared to
be an adventure turned to terror. To enter where we
could view the colonies of slumbering bats required us
to slither on our stomachs through narrow slices in the
rock. My friend assured me that once inside we could
stand—and that the flashlights had brand new
batteries! I would only have entered that cave bound,
gagged and dragged. I don't recall what we did do that
day, but fear kept me from entering the cave.

Trappist monk Thomas Merton concluded in *New
Seeds of Contemplation*, "The poet enters into himself to
create. The contemplative enters into God in order to be
created." Francis of Assisi had the heart of a
contemplative. Before he could begin to rebuild the
Church, Francis had to be rebuilt himself. His
experiences—dreaming of Lady Poverty, being called
from the crucifix and severing himself from all that had
previously held value in his life—led him to serious
self-doubt. Was he following God or was he going
crazy? God did not provide Francis with a daily
itinerary of how to follow his new calling. And so
Francis had to enter into the cave of himself in order to
become the person God had called him to be.

Caves pock the Umbrian hills. Some appear like a
gentle giant's thumbprints in the stony slopes. Others
slice the mountainside, seemingly axed into the rock.
Recently the trails around the Carceri, the caves Francis

frequented near Assisi, have been marked with signs indicating the presence of snakes in the area. Pilgrims to the sites have undoubtedly been surprised by God's less beloved creations.

Francis plunged into the caves in search of self and God. In these womb-like mountain chambers he was separated from what had previously attracted him— comfort, fun, gatherings of friends, success. When one plunges into something, he has no way of knowing how deep he might go. Plunging, whether into deep water or on a bungee cord, is risk-taking. Some risk-taking is foolhardy; other risks are essential for exploring opportunities in life.

Caves are sprinkled through Judeo-Christian tradition. Elijah found God in the gentle breeze that ruffled past his cave hideaway (see 1 Kings 19:11-13a). Mary's womb was like an empty cave until filled by the power of the Holy Spirit. Jesus was born in a cave converted into a stable and buried in another cave, in which he rose from the dead. Most caves are lightless empty spaces in encompassing places.

Francis fled to the caves above Assisi to discover himself and his God. The vehicle for his inward journey was prayer. Here in the cave he was alone with God. Here God's message was not dimmed by the din of critical voices: "Francis is a fool!" "Francis is an ungrateful son!" He was not tempted by the taunting of old friends, "Come out with us tonight, old friend! We're planning a grand party!" In the dark of the caves Francis plunged deeply into the spiritual darkness of his own doubt. The light of God's love showed him the way he was to follow. And, for the remainder of his life, whenever Francis was discouraged, confused, wondering if he was really following God, he returned to the caves to pray, to find his way.

I once invited a friend to join me on retreat. She responded, "I did that in high school" (many years ago!) "and I won't do it again!" As we discussed her adamant feelings about her retreat experience, she explained that during that earlier retreat she had actually felt God calling her to a new way of life. She liked the life she had and refused to sacrifice it. Now, years later, she still refused to enter the "cave" of a retreat for fear she might hear from God again.

A spiritual retreat is just one kind of cave experience we might encounter to move away from distractions that obscure our communication with God. Other possibilities are endless. We may seek God while sitting in a special chair in the corner of a bedroom, a closet, the barn or garage, in a quiet place in a park or yard, a desk at work, in a chapel or church, under the cellar stairs—wherever we can reach into the darkness of ourselves and discover God's light is a potential cave.

One busy mother's cave was her apron. She pulled the apron over her head as she sat in a kitchen chair when she needed to return to God in prayer. Her family recognized this was a time to give her peace and quiet.

As a child, I retreated to the cool quiet of a bowered forsythia bush on warm summer days. I would not have said I was seeking God, but years later, I recognize those trips into the greenery as journeys into self to discovery of God.

If we can bless ourselves with extended time in a

quiet cave of prayer, we may be astonished at the reward. It takes time to relinquish the thoughts and concerns of daily life, to release ourselves to God, to quiet our spirits enough to hear God speak in the silence of our minds and hearts. We need time to stir up willingness to allow God to reveal our need for conversion.

For Francis, diving into the cave of prayer left him spiritually breathless. He would, while in prayer, seek refuge on imaginary "shelves" in the walls of his interior cavern. After regaining his spiritual breath, Francis would leave the security of that stopping point and begin to plunge again into himself. His quest was to discard whatever might separate him from God and to discover what might draw him closer.

As we dive deeper into God's presence, we divest ourselves of what is superfluous. Unnecessary attitudes, worries, fears and angers float to the surface to be carried away by God's loving care. What we discover, as Francis realized, is that God is not in the trappings in which we have enshrined God, but within us.

The Canticle

Francis' song of praise to God reveals Francis' response to all that God is to him and to the world.

The Canticle of Brother Sun

Most high, all-powerful, all good, Lord!
  All praise is yours, all glory, all honour
  And all blessing.
To you, alone, Most High, do they belong.
  No mortal lips are worthy

To pronounce your name.

All praise be yours, my Lord, through all that you have
    made,
 And first my lord Brother Sun,
  Who brings the day; and light you give to us through
    him.
How beautiful is he, how radiant in all his splendour!
  Of you, Most High, he bears the likeness.

All praise be yours, my Lord, through Sister Moon and
    Stars;
  In the heavens you have made them, bright
  And precious and fair.

All praise be yours, my Lord, through Brothers Wind
    and Air,
  And fair and stormy, all the weather's moods,
  By which you cherish all that you have made.

All praise be yours, my Lord, through Sister Water,
  So useful, lowly, precious and pure.

All praise be yours, my Lord, through Brother Fire,
  Through whom you brighten up the night.
  How beautiful is he, how gay! Full of power and
    strength.

All praise be yours, my Lord, through Sister Earth, our
    mother,
  Who feeds us in her sovereignty and produces
  Various fruits with coloured flowers and herbs.

All praise be yours, my Lord, through those who grant
    pardon
  For love of you; through those who endure
  Sickness and trial.
Happy those who endure in peace,

By you, Most High, they will be crowned.

All praise be yours, my Lord, through Sister Death,
  From whose embrace no mortal can escape.
  Woe to those who die in mortal sin!
  Happy those She finds doing your will!
  The second death can do no harm to them.
Praise and bless my Lord, and give him thanks,
  And serve him with great humility.

The canticle sings in simple words of praise all that Francis discovered of the glory and goodness of God. All he discovered through visions in his early conversion, from the words from the crucifix of San Damiano, his pummeling of God in prayer in the caves, his experiences of the brotherhood of lesser brothers, his own illness and approaching death—all is distilled to praise.

Each path Francis took on his journey to God led him to a single action: praise of God. Through the entire domain of earth, from the glory of daybreak to nightfall's softened light, Francis praises the Lord. Through all weather, the elements of fire and water and the motherhood of the earth, Francis continues in praise. Sickness and trial give birth to continuing praise. The inevitable encounter with Sister Death spurs Francis to close his work with praise, blessing and thanksgiving. Everything that happened in Francis' life fueled the fire of his praise to the Lord.

Francis leaves us with a legacy of praise. If we claim it as our heritage, we must use it as Francis did—in every circumstance of life without reservation. "But," we think, "I can't praise God for my father's

Alzheimer's disease." "How can I praise God for joblessness? For debilitating illness? For the pain and grief that thunder through my life?" Francis, like the Lord he followed, teaches us to praise God *through* the trials that enter every life. Only then can we experience release from the bonds of anguish and despair. If we release our deepest emotions to God, we defuse their power to create havoc in our lives.

As she slipped and fell next to her car on an icy January morning, Aileen said aloud, "Praise the Lord!" The woman stepping from the next car was surprised by the elderly woman's words at a time that did not seem praiseworthy to her. As they sought care for the resulting broken arm, Aileen shared her view of praise. "If I hadn't praised God, I would probably have chastised myself for being so clumsy. Or I might have criticized the store management for not tending the parking lot better. I'm sure I would have felt more pain because I would have been angry and focused on myself. Praise somehow sets things right with God and with me."

Praise works! We may never understand in this life how, but it does work wonders.

Francis shows us the way to praise. If his way seems impossible, consider this story. Before my mother and I visited Assisi we discussed the places we would see. I commented, "There is one thing we will not do— climb to the top of Mount Subasio." Though plucky and a great walker, my mom was in her mid-seventies.

After checking into the guest house, we began to explore the town that is grafted to the side of the mountain. Winding streets, meandering stairways and paths transform walking tours into adventures. We found a path that looked interesting and ventured along it. As it gently wound upward, we realized it had no byways or side roads. Foliage obscured the view up and the view down. Finally at a bend the view from the path broke open. Where were we? Nearly at the top of Mount Subasio, of course!

It had seemed too difficult when we contemplated climbing to the top. But done in blind faith that we were going somewhere, it was an easily accomplished task. And we praised God for the journey.

Learning to praise God through all the events that life confronts us with may seem like an impossible task. In reality, all we have to do is begin to follow the path of praise. God will lead us on.

The Stigmata

The wounds of Christ that Francis received on La Verna mark him forever as a prayer himself, a word of God spoken on earth.

"Passion loves company" proclaims a highway billboard. The words are superimposed upon a muted image of a luxury car with the dealer's name in smaller letters below. The advertisement speaks loud and clear about what has become the "passion" of our culture. The luxury car represents only one aspect of that kind of passion. It could have been a championship sports team, a perfect human body, clothes "to kill for," as a logo claims. Even those who cannot possess the items they long for continue to desire them "passionately."

A string of synonyms for *passion* stream from the thesaurus: "appetite, desire, hunger, lust, ardor, emotion, fervor, intensity, craving, obsession, yearning, affection, fancy, infatuation, love." Few of these words blend with a spiritual concept of passion. That void offers a clue that the world's concept of passion differs greatly from a Christian's view. The Passion of Christ as he submitted to the judgment of others and his own death on the cross renders a meaning for the word *passion* that is far beyond our comprehension.

For nearly two millennia the faithful have attempted to wrap their minds and hearts around the essence of Christ's Passion. Contemplating that event is difficult because of the pain it involves when its meaning penetrates our hearts. Contemplating Christ's Passion produces fear: What if we are asked to share in that Passion in the events of our own lives? What if we cannot say yes? What if we have no choice?

Yet the message of the highway billboard's words is accurate: Passion loves company. Jesus' Passion was the ultimate sacrifice of love—unstinting, sacrificial love for God and for God's people. The question is: Are we willing to accompany Jesus along a way of life that may lead to that kind of passion?

I shudder when I consider what that might mean in my life. *Sacrifice* is not the most popular word in the American vocabulary. Its redemptive significance is lost in times that say, "Not in my backyard!" to facilities for mentally ill people, AIDS patients, drug rehabilitation programs, homes for unwed mothers. Sacrifice is incomprehensible to those who strive to be Number One at any cost. Sacrifice is unfathomable when self-gratification is a life goal.

Francis never saw that billboard, but he lived its

message: "Passion loves company." Francis chose to accompany Christ in a passionately sacrificial way of life. He loved everyone and everything in creation with a love so consuming that it devoured him physically and emotionally so that he might grow spiritually. He gave and gave, asking for nothing in return. Perhaps one of his greatest acts of sacrificial love is the one that is hardest to understand—sacrificing his relationship with his earthly father so that he could say without reservation, "My Father who art in heaven!" That action did not indicate that Francis failed to love his earthly father. It meant that he was willing to sacrifice even that relationship if it stood in the way of a greater one.

How might we define *passion*? As love beyond human comprehension? As loving sacrifice of whatever we hold dear in order to be true to the highest love? *Passion* is a word to ponder. It is, as a seminary professor loved to say, "a thought for the shower"—or better still, a thought for the cave of our prayers.

Francis' decision to keep company with Jesus in his Passion was formed by a myriad of choices: to fall in love with Lady Poverty; to turn from war to nurturing a peaceful spirit, to pivot between steeping his life in prayer and helping the poor, the sick and the suffering. Francis could never have guessed that his choices would lead to a physical realization of the Passion of Christ in his own body. He could only request in repeated prayer that he be permitted the honor of sharing the agony of his beloved Savior.

His prayer was answered. One September day two years before his death, Francis ascended Mount La Verna. Perhaps he wanted to climb above the strife in the world below. Maybe he felt, as we may be inclined to feel, closer to God in high places. A cave was there— a place to delve into the recesses of his own spirit, to untangle the emotions and questions that mingled in his life.

God had anointed Francis throughout his life of conversion. God had touched Francis' mind with the vision of Lady Poverty and hallowed his hearing with the words from the San Damiano crucifix. God had dedicated Francis' mouth to speaking the gospel in a way that brought it to life in those who had forgotten how to live God's way. God had ordained Francis' hands to cleanse the horrendous sores of leprosy. God had sanctified Francis' prayer with power to rebuild the Church of Christendom. Now God would consecrate the frail and ailing body of this faithful servant.

Even as a handsome man-like seraph with six wings and bearing the marks of crucifixion approached him, Francis could not anticipate what was happening. Fear and joy compounded his confusion. As Francis struggled with the anxiety that rose within him, his hands and feet were pierced as if by nails. A wound appeared on his right side. The crucified Christ now had the company of one who loved him beyond all reason, with all passion.

And so Francis would live the remainder of his life marked by the signs of his total consecration to God. He would hide the painful, bleeding wounds. To allow others to see them threatened to diminish the intimacy of God's touch upon his body.

Life is full of human acts of amazing sacrificial love. Parents sacrifice for their children. Rescuers risk all to save lost climbers. Heroic actions bring others from the brink of death. Sisters and brothers donate organs to save siblings. Passersby challenge flames in a burning house to rescue sleeping children. Sometimes those who give of themselves are marked with the wounds of their sacrifice—injuries, scars, burns, even loss of life. Sometimes the wounds are hidden deep within.

You and I know many stories of those who bring the story of sacrificial, passionate love to life. But those may be other people's stories. What is important is for us to consider the way in which your life and mine might follow Francis, who became Saint Francis of Assisi because of his passionate love for God.

Will we choose to try at least a slow dance with Lady Poverty? She will not rob us of what we do not choose to surrender to her love. Perhaps we will risk a venture into the cave of prayer, a dive into the core of our innermost self to discover who really lives there.

If we choose to make God our God and our all, we may find as Francis did that we are not alone with God but in the company of thousands who, following our example, join in the journey. As we read the daily newspaper or watch the evening news, the Spirit moving within us may breathe, "My God and my all!" We have no hope but God. But no greater hope is possible than God.

Francis called himself the herald of a great king. Many still have not heard the trumpet blast announcing that the great king has come and will come again. We, too, can be heralds for the great king, Jesus. We can herald his presence in our lives through acts that reveal in our flesh that "passion loves company."

Conclusion

IF YOU HAVE READ to this point of this book and are thinking, "This sounds like plain Christianity to me," Saint Francis of Assisi would be overjoyed! That is precisely what Franciscan spirituality is—simple, plain Christianity. "[I]t is no longer I who live, but it is Christ who lives in me. And the life I now live in the flesh I live by faith in the Son of God, who loved me and gave himself for me. I do not nullify the grace of God..." (Galatians 2:20-21a).

Through the centuries the faithful have encumbered Christianity with many gifts offered in love to their faith. Unfortunately, some of those religious practices begin to obscure the heart of our faith. The situation is similar to a loving family in which parents and grandparents give too much to the children they love. Soon the children are burdened with too many options, too many toys, too many opportunities. They experience difficulty knowing who they really are. If these children, who are truly loved, cannot identify themselves without all the trappings, they lose their ability to develop into the individuals God has created them to become.

Following Francis—which means following

Christ—means peeling the cultural layers from Christianity. In doing so we strip away nonessential layers of inculturation imposed over the centuries. We rediscover the Christ who loves us so much that he will share his passionate love for all of God's creation with us if only we say yes.

What are the elements of Franciscan spirituality that transcend the boundaries of the medieval life of Francis and invade the present?

Francis took God very seriously; he did not regard himself seriously. We follow Francis because he was totally human as he followed Christ. Christ is the one we really follow, but it is so tempting to say, "But he was God! I can't do what he did." But Francis *did* live as Jesus instructs. Francis took Christianity on the road in Europe, Africa and the Near East. Imagine where we can take Christ in our mobile society. Corporate towers, not church spires, now dominate city skylines. The challenge for Franciscans in the world is to infuse those corporate domains, our homes, bowling alleys and grocery stores, schools and factories with "Franchristian spirituality"—Christian life lived in the simplicity and love of Saint Francis of Assisi. "Thy kingdom come, thy will be done on earth as it is in heaven," we pray. A frequent error is to neglect "on earth" as we focus on heaven.

The time to begin is now. As Francis himself said, "...[T]here was no one to tell me what I should do; but the Most High himself made it clear to me that I must live the life of the gospel" (*The Testament of St. Francis*).

Resources

For information about the Secular Franciscan Order, call 1-800-FRANCIS.

Books

Anthony, Edd, O.F.M. *Canticle of Brother Sun.* Cincinnati, Ohio: St. Anthony Messenger Press and Franciscan Communications, 1989.

Armstrong, Regis J., O.F.M. Cap., and Brady, Ignatius, O.F.M. *Francis and Clare: The Complete Works*, The Classics of Western Spirituality. New York: Paulist Press, 1982.

Bodo, Murray, O.F.M. *Francis: The Journey and the Dream.* Cincinnati, Ohio: St. Anthony Messenger Press, 1988.

_____. *Francisco: El Viaje y el Sueno.* Cincinnati, Ohio: St. Anthony Messenger Press, 1994.

_____. *Tales of St. Francis: Ancient Stories for Contemporary Living.* Cincinnati, Ohio: St. Anthony Messenger Press, 1992.

_____. *Through the Year With Francis of Assisi.* Cincinnati, Ohio: St. Anthony Messenger Press, 1993.

_____. *The Way of St. Francis: The Challenge of Franciscan Spirituality for Everyone*. Cincinnati, Ohio: St. Anthony Messenger Press, 1995.

Bodo, Murray, O.F.M., and Susan Saint Sing. *A Retreat With Francis and Clare of Assisi: Following Our Pilgrim Hearts*. Cincinnati, Ohio: St. Anthony Messenger Press, 1996.

Chesterton, G. K. *St. Francis of Assisi*. New York: George H. Doran Co., 1924.

Cook, William R. *Francis of Assisi: The Way of Poverty and Humility*. Wilmington, Del.: Michael Glazier, 1989.

Fortini, Arnaldo. *Francis of Assisi*. New York: Seabury, 1980.

Haase, Albert. *Swimming in the Sun: Discovering the Lord's Prayer With Francis of Assisi and Thomas Merton*. Cincinnati, Ohio: St. Anthony Messenger Press, 1993.

Habig, Marion, ed. *St. Francis of Assisi: Writings and Early Biographies: English Omnibus of the Sources for the Life of St. Francis*. Chicago: Franciscan Herald Press, 1973.

Holl, Adolf. *The Last Christian*. New York: Doubleday, 1980.

Hutchinson, Gloria. *Six Ways to Pray From Six Great Saints*. Cincinnati, Ohio: St. Anthony Messenger Press, 1982.

Leclerc, Eloi. *Wisdom of the Poverello*. Chicago: Franciscan Herald Press, 1989.

Moorman, John R. H. *Richest of Poor Men: The Spirituality of St. Francis of Assisi.* Huntington, Ind.: Our Sunday Visitor, 1977.

Noonan, Hugh, O.F.M., and Roy Gasnick, O.F.M. *Francis of Assisi: The Song Goes On.* Cincinnati, Ohio: St. Anthony Messenger Press and Franciscan Communications, 1994.

Pazzelli, Raffael. *St. Francis and The Third Order.* Chicago: Franciscan Herald Press, 1989.

Audiocassettes

Harkins, Conrad, O.F.M. *Francis of Assisi: Enduring Values.* Cincinnati, Ohio: St. Anthony Messenger Press, 1995.

Rohr, Richard, O.F.M. *Letting Go: A Spirituality of Subtraction.* Cincinnati, Ohio: St. Anthony Messenger Press, 1987.

_____. *Rebuild the Church.* Cincinnati, Ohio: St. Anthony Messenger Press, 1994.

Video

Hodgson, Karen. *Clare of Assisi,* Oblate Media. Distributed by St. Anthony Messenger Press. Senior high to adult.

St. Francis of Assisi. Distributed by St. Anthony Messenger Press. All ages.

Sbicca, Arturo. *St. Clare of Assisi,* Oriente Occidente Productions. Distributed by St. Anthony Messenger

Press. Junior high to adult.

_____. *St. Francis of Assisi*, Oriente Occidente Productions. Distributed by St. Anthony Messenger Press. Junior high to adult.

The Message of St. Francis for Today, with Michael Crosby, O.F.M. Cap. Fisher Productions, Box 727, Jefferson Valley, NY 10535; phone: 914-245-8509, fax: 914-245-1354. Distributed by St. Anthony Messenger Press.